GERRARD'S
BLUEPRINT

ADAM THORNTON

GERRARD'S
BLUEPRINT

The Tactical Philosophy Behind
Rangers 55th Title Triumph

First published by Pitch Publishing, 2022

Pitch Publishing
9 Donnington Park,
85 Birdham Road,
Chichester,
West Sussex,
PO20 7AJ
www.pitchpublishing.co.uk
info@pitchpublishing.co.uk

ISBN 978 1 80150 057 9

Typesetting and origination by Pitch Publishing
Printed and bound in India by Replika Press Pvt. Ltd.

Contents

For Lynn, Rosie and Raya. Thank you for putting up with me and for your support throughout this process. I couldn't have done this without you.

Introduction

FIRST AND foremost, I am a Rangers fan. My first season ticket was in the Govan Rear in 1994 – the year Rangers signed Brian Laudrup from Fiorentina six years into the quest for nine in a row. Not a bad time to start the Rangers love affair, was it?

Some 24 years later, in May 2018, Liverpool legend Steven Gerrard was appointed Rangers manager and tasked with returning the club to the top of the Scottish pile. The disastrous events of 2012 had seen Rangers demoted to League Two and left with no alternative but to climb back to the top division.

I have poured every emotion felt during Gerrard's three full seasons at Rangers into this book, and I dearly hope that the love I have for football in general but, more importantly, for our great club shines through on every page.

I've also spent the last four years as the host of *Tactics Talk* – a podcast on the Heart and Hand Network which attempts to analyse and dissect Rangers' tactical philosophy before and throughout Gerrard's reign as manager. This book is the culmination of everything I've learned about Rangers' approach under Gerrard at every step of the journey, from that first Europa League qualifier against FK Shkupi on 12 July 2018 all the way to clinching the title in record time on 7 March 2021.

During this tumultuous three-year period, the podcast was a cathartic experience for myself and my co-host Alistair Bain. Throughout this, we attempted to make sense of what was – or perhaps was not – happening on the pitch and tried to understand the rollercoaster journey we had all been on. I would also like to thank Ally, as his knowledge of football, coaching, tactics, and dedication to his craft is massively inspiring to an amateur enthusiast like me. He has helped me improve my knowledge and understanding of football to a much deeper level than before.

This book will document my understanding of Steven Gerrard's blueprint for Rangers by identifying the critical overarching principles of his tactics. It will also attempt to chart the evolution of Rangers' approach on a season-by-season basis over the three years as the visual embodiment of this philosophy. In my opinion, there were clear and noticeable incremental tactical improvements in each of those seasons, and the intention is to capture all of them on the journey to once again being crowned Scottish league champions.

As football fans, we love to talk about formations and tactics, even without realising we're doing it at times. We endlessly discuss whether Rangers should go back to the 4-4-2 glory days under Graeme Souness in the late 1980s or possibly variations of the three-man defences utilised in the '90s by Walter Smith and Dick Advocaat. We yearn for the free-flowing 4-2-4 formation associated with Rangers' last treble win in 2002/03 under Alex McLeish.

The word formation as a descriptor has almost become a proxy to attempt to articulate a playing style when in reality, most teams may change shape several times within the same game depending on the situation. How a team lines up on a TV screen pre-game – usually with one or two players listed in the wrong position – is a tiny part of a much more detailed story. Essentially, a team formation is too restrictive and lacks the nuance to give a detailed enough indication of the way they play. The word shape is a more contextual descriptor, as a team's shape can be dynamic and fluid depending on in-game situations and each team's overarching approach.

This book will not solely be focused on tactical theory and philosophy. The essential part of any football team is the players who cross that white line week in, week out and give their best for the cause. The group of Rangers players analysed throughout this book will go down in history as legends for their achievements in season 2020/21, and rightly so. Still, they didn't arrive fully formed in the summer of 2020 – never mind two years previously – ready to claim their crown. They, too, went through considerable evolutions – some much more than others – and they are the fundamental elements of this story.

We know that Rangers' full-backs were a vital weapon for the team, adding width and vast amounts of creativity. Still, James Tavernier and Borna Barišić would admit that they embarked on a significant journey throughout these three years to get to the stage of being crowned league champions. The central midfield three in Gerrard's first game against Shkupi consisted of Ross McCrorie, Daniel Candeias and Scott Arfield. Looking at arguably the most complex and detailed evolution within the team, I will attempt to illustrate the stages of development in the centre of the pitch and delve deep into the key players who contributed heavily along the way.

And what of Alfredo Morelos? A promising if inconsistent 21-year-old striker when Gerrard took over, his evolution was arguably the most considerable over the three years and resulted in the Colombian becoming Rangers' all-time top European goalscorer following his goal against Benfica in November 2020. The management team also added footballers of significant calibre incrementally. We'll look at players such as Filip Helander, Steven Davis and Kemar Roofe and how their signings improved the overall quality and also necessitated tactical tweaks to benefit the team.

All of these and more will be covered throughout the second half of this book as we dig deep into the analysis of the key players and discuss their tactical roles within the team. Allied to that, we will discuss their strengths and weaknesses and explain how this combined perfectly into the winning machine we saw throughout 2020/21.

As I wrote this book during a global pandemic, it would be remiss of me not to discuss this period's impact on Rangers. From a strictly footballing perspective, Rangers were in a bad way when the world, including football, shut down. As the players trudged off the field on 8 March 2020 after a scrappy 1-0 win against Ross County in the league, the world had no idea what would unfold in the months to come. The 2-1 victory over Celtic in the customary new year Old Firm derby at Parkhead on 28 December 2019 was a massive boost as it brought Rangers to within two points of Celtic with a game in hand as Scotland shut down for the winter break. Upon their return in late January, Rangers would accumulate just 17 points from their next 10 games, leaving them 13 behind Celtic with a game in hand when the pandemic ceased play. This book won't dip into the detail of why the 2019/20 league season didn't restart in Scotland as it did in pretty much every other nation in the world. Instead, it will analyse the detail behind how Gerrard and his coaching staff used this extended period of downtime to extraordinary effect.

Fast forward from 8 March 2020 to 15 May 2021, a mere 433 days later, and who could have foreseen that Rangers would be league champions? Not only that, but that they would remain unbeaten for every single league game, conceding just 13 league goals and breaking the British league record set by José Mourinho's all-conquering Chelsea team of 2004/05?

Such a beautiful story, and here's how it goes.

Part 1

Tactical Philosophy

Tactical Influences

'If you look at the deliberations we had around managers, there are a lot of boxes that one tries to tick and no one ticks all of the boxes,' then Rangers chairman Dave King told *The Herald*.

'When Mark [Allen, Rangers' director of football] first said to me about Steven Gerrard as a potential manager, my first thought was clearly that he hadn't managed before.

'But that is the only box that he didn't tick. Every other box he did tick.

'Competitive ability, a winner, knows what it takes to win – so he was ticking all the boxes other than experience.'

When King announced the appointment of Gerrard to the media on 4 May 2018, he famously remarked above that the only skill that Gerrard didn't have was the experience as a manager. After his short period in charge of Liverpool's under-18 and under-19 teams, Rangers fans had no idea how a Gerrard team would line up or how he wanted his side to play football.

While the Rangers job was Gerrard's first foray into first-team management, there had been some opportunities to dip his toe in the water before his time coaching at Liverpool's academy. In November 2016, while still in the last days of his hugely successful playing career, he had tentative discussions to take over as manager at Milton Keynes Dons but elected not to on that occasion. There was a minimal frame of reference, but the experience can come in many ways, as Gerrard outlined when speaking to the Rangers Coaches Convention following the conclusion of his third season in charge in May 2021.

Speaking to the Rangers website, Gerrard was asked if there was a specific point in his career where he realised that coaching or management was where he saw his career going when he decided to hang up his boots, Gerrard said, 'It was more towards the back end of my career, but when you get the responsibility of being a captain, you're already doing little bits and bobs of being a manager anyway. Talking to people one to one, trying to help them whether that's on the pitch tactically or off the pitch where you're showing them support. It's your type of character that leads you in that direction anyway. In terms of coaching badges and qualifications, it was probably towards my late 20s, early 30s where I thought this might be something that interests me further down the line.'

Clearly, Gerrard felt that his role as captain helped prepare him for the job in certain ways. Still, ultimately his ability to translate his ideas on to the coaching pitch and have players buy into his philosophy would be critical to any potential success. It was abundantly clear from the very early months of Gerrard's time at Ibrox just how much influence the 'Liverpool DNA' has had on his and his coaching staff's view on football. Having been in the Liverpool system for almost 30 years as a boy, man and captain, this will come as no surprise to anyone. But knowing these principles is one thing; implementing them is quite another.

During his brief time in charge of Liverpool's under-18s, he learned and adapted quickly and visualised how he saw himself as a coach and manager. Gerrard told the Rangers website of his philosophy, 'It wouldn't make sense [to him] if you decided to go with a philosophy that you started fresh when you finished your career. Mine was built from the DNA of Liverpool and being around top internationals. I learned a lot of principles and values, and I was lucky enough to lead at under-18 and under-19 level. That was an opportunity for me to try different formations, different systems, different ways of playing, but I was always wanting to stick to that DNA which was always to be a possession-based team in terms of owning the ball.'

Within Gerrard's 'own the pitch, own the ball' philosophy, he identified certain principles that he felt should symbolise any team he coached in the future. These included always playing one-touch football, moving the ball quickly and playing with tempo and intensity. Another critical theme woven through is how aggressive Gerrard wants his teams to be when out of possession but embedded within a tight structure. If you implement a high pressing structure, you must ensure the whole team remains aligned when the press is initiated. To do this, the team must stay compact and tight and move around the pitch in units to ensure maximum coverage should the pressure fail and the opposition exploit an opportunity to attack.

Gerrard went on to say, 'The biggest learning curve for me with my philosophy is not to be set on one thing because you need to be adaptable within your philosophy to certain challenges and contrasting games but if I stay true to my values and the DNA I've built in Liverpool, I believed that would work at Rangers too.'

King's comments about Gerrard's lack of first-hand managerial experience were, of course, correct in the literal sense. Still, as outlined, he did have over 16 years' experience of top-level football while being exposed to elite-level tactical formations, ideas and structures during his time as the midfield lynchpin for Liverpool and England. Indeed, Gerrard's first 12 years as a professional at Liverpool were spent entirely under the tutelage of two of the greatest tactical minds of the last 25 years in Gérard Houllier and Rafa Benítez.

'I have tapped into them all, Rafa, Brendan [Rodgers], Gérard Houllier, Roy Hodgson, all of them,' he told the *Liverpool Echo*. 'What would Rafa have said to us in that situation? What would Brendan have said in and out of possession? So, you try and take things from them all.'

Gerrard was a guest on ex-Liverpool team-mate Jamie Carragher's *The Greatest Game* podcast in early 2020, where he provided some more meat on the bone in terms of the influences that have shaped his style.

'In terms of tactics, I always try to go to Rafa for the base out of possession and what we learned. [To be] compact, the block, no lines sliding, quick at moving the ball and, depending on who you are playing, do you go back to a low block or a medium block? It's not that Rafa was negative but I want to have a little bit more than that because if I have dreams and aims of coaching at the top and at big clubs like Rangers, you have to have an exciting team and play in a certain way where you go for teams out of possession and, when you get it, have exciting players. Otherwise I'm just not sure the fans will have you for that long.'

Another key facet of Gerrard's style is Rangers' approach to pressing and counter-pressing in a concerted, well-disciplined manner. There are definite shades of Jürgen Klopp's gegenpressing style in the way they aggressively hunt in packs to try to win the ball back quickly after losing it.

A few months after being appointed as manager, Gerrard revealed he was 'like a sponge' under Klopp at Liverpool and while there are many tactical similarities between both teams, there is also a mental aspect which Gerrard seems to value more than others. Famed for wearing his heart on his sleeve as a player, this carried on into his early years at Rangers with his emotional side bared to the world on more than one occasion, for better or worse.

'In terms of management, I've tried to be a sponge and steal things from all the managers I've played for,' he told *The Scotsman*. 'I've tapped into loads of that education in this Rangers journey, especially in Europe and the top games, we have played domestically.

'I've stolen stuff from Brendan Rodgers and Sven-Göran Eriksson in terms of the style and how it looks, playing through the lines and building from the back.

'It's important to be yourself when you are in these roles and do it your way. But I've worked with top managers and coaches, so I'd be a fool not to try and steal and use their expertise for my benefit.

'It's important for me not to nail myself to one philosophy and make a liar out of myself.

'Because I think it all depends on what your job is, where you are working, what league you are in. So, for example, this is my first job here at Rangers. If my philosophy was a low block, hard to play against, we soak it up and play on the counter-attack – that doesn't work in every game.'

Shortly after Rangers secured the Scottish Premiership title in 2021, Gerrard spoke to the *Mirror* of Klopp's influence in their brief time together at Liverpool.

'One thing I learned from Jürgen is to try and detach yourself, and be more balanced around the results,' he said.

'He is a master of it. I am not. I am trying to get better at it. I was an emotional player, and I wore my heart on my sleeve. I feel results and want to be as authentic and real as I can.

'But as a manager you have to be more balanced.'

Gerrard and his staff did a lot of work on the training pitch with the supporters in mind. They were aware of the traditions of clubs like Rangers, and there were constant references to the supporters' demands and how the team should play needs to align to that. Rangers have to have a specific philosophy that aligns with the fans' expectations. They will not accept a team that primarily play defensive, hard-to-beat football and try to break on the counter. The team must always play attacking and aggressive football fused with grit, hard work and determination. These are the traditions Rangers is built on, and the coaching staff were able to tap into their experience at Liverpool to embed these principles in the squad from an early stage.

As outlined, this was a collaborative team effort; therefore, when we speak about the tactical influences that have shaped this Rangers team, we must also talk about the coaches who have shaped Michael Beale's philosophy.

Like Gerrard, first-team coach Beale has been heavily influenced by clubs he has worked for and coaches he has worked with during his 20-year career.

Having grown up in 1990s London, Beale's fascination with football is similar to most of the same age, dominated by the Premier League and Serie A. Such was the exposure to the Italian game via the excellent *Football Italia* on Channel 4, there are many of us with long-lasting *calcio* obsessions.

Given Beale's love for English football and his keen eye on the foreign game, it is no surprise that Sir Bobby Robson was one of the biggest influences on him as a young coach. He describes Sir Bobby as a 'trailblazer for English coaches' due to his time coaching clubs such as Barcelona, Sporting Lisbon, Porto and PSV, as well as the England national team. Beale also held a long-term desire to coach abroad one day, which would be realised with his brief spell as assistant manager at São Paulo.

Another name frequently features when Beale discusses his influences: Johan Cruyff, or the man he calls 'the most important person in the history of football'. On his website, Beale describes his playing style as being one he revered and how much he valued Cruyff's thoughts on how football should be played at a more cerebral level during his time at Ajax and Barcelona.

Two more massive names in European football come up time and time again when Beale talks about his footballing philosophy, and both are coaches he worked with during his time at Chelsea's academy. Firstly, Carlo Ancelotti has played and coached at the highest level for 40 years in numerous major European leagues, winning domestic titles and three Champions Leagues. This adaptability to new surroundings, allied to his incredible man-management skills, is key to his longevity as a manager. Indeed, the 4-3-2-1 system that Rangers have used throughout Gerrard and Beale's time at the club shares more than a few similarities with the Champions League-winning AC Milan teams of the early to mid-2000s, managed by none other than Ancelotti.

Secondly, José Mourinho is admired as a manager who was outstanding on the training pitch. In an article on his website, Beale details how stunned he was at the attention to detail throughout sessions and how the coaches worked seamlessly together to provide players with an elite training environment and platform to succeed on the pitch. He references Mourinho as key in his understanding of what was required to one day reach that level as a coach himself.

In over two decades of coaching in professional football clubs to date, Beale spent 12 years in development roles at Chelsea and Liverpool's academies. As such, he is influenced by developing young players and places a tremendous amount of focus on that despite moving fully into first-team environments thereafter at São Paulo first and now at Rangers.

One key theme running through any interview with Beale is his belief in how important the players and environment are to a team's success. His opinion is that players win you games, and formations and tactics are always secondary to that.

The Management Team

'When you take a job, it's important you get the right people around you who will complement your skillset. This will help to make a really effective and good coaching team, and I believe I've got that here,' said Gerrard, speaking on the *Robbie Fowler Podcast* in February 2021.

'What I'll never do is try and do someone's job who is better than me at doing that job.

'For example, I'd been working on a coaching team behind the scenes when I'd been manager of Liverpool's under-18s and 19s for some time.

'People wouldn't believe how close I'd been watching certain people to take with me when the opportunity eventually came.

'But, what I do is make sure I'm there for every session and make sure I'm in the middle of every session. If I feel I need to step in then I will.

'If I need to take a part of the session, I'll do that. I'm always around the team shape – how I want it to look in and out of possession.

'But I won't overtake everyone and stand on people's toes and then by the time Saturday three o'clock comes the players are sick of my voice, sick of my face and after six months no players want to play for you.

'So, it's about understanding my skillsets and how they work on a weekly schedule and how everyone works around that to make sure that we've got the right pieces in the right places and I must say my staff have been incredible for me.

'They've been on every single session. They've lived the journey with me and I've got total belief and confidence in them. I see this as a relationship and a group for a long time, if that's what they want as well.'

Steven Gerrard was the Rangers manager. In many ways, the word manager can be perceived differently depending on your viewpoint. For some, a manager will always be immersed in every facet of a club. The ultimate owner of coaching the first team, overseeing the scouting process and dealing with the press. Legends of the British game such as Walter Smith or Alex Ferguson always immediately spring to mind when you hear the word manager. This role has changed and evolved somewhat throughout the last 10 or 15 years, with 'head coach' roles becoming more prevalent in European football.

The head coach at most clubs, but not all, has a much more streamlined role than in previous years, being tasked primarily with coaching the first team throughout the week and leading them into games. They certainly still retain an input and influence into a club's scouting strategy, the process of signing players and an interest in the overall financial affairs. Still, they are not the owner of these areas in the way they once were. As the game of football has exploded in popularity worldwide and has become ever more complex, roles and responsibilities have been tweaked or split in ways that allow more specialists and fewer generalists to come to the fore. In the top five leagues and beyond, it is now more common to NOT have a sporting director/director of football responsible for the entire football department at a club. Often, the head coach or manager will report directly or indirectly to them.

The consensus is that a manager's job is relatively temporary in the modern game and heavily depends on factors outside the club's control. A poor run of results – or conversely, an awe-inspiring run – can and does see managers regularly leaving their post within a few months. It stands to reason then that hiring a manager plus his backroom staff and signing an entire squad of players precisely to fit this manager's style may not have been the best long-term approach for clubs to take in the past. The director of football role should have that long-term view, a senior executive of the club responsible for setting the vision and hiring coaches and players as he sees fit to deliver this.

When Gerrard was appointed, Mark Allen was in his post as director of football at Rangers, having joined in the season prior. There were some missteps in the transfer market, with some players brought in who, at first glance, didn't quite seem to fit the style of play the manager was implementing. Still, overall, the process worked well in those first two transfer windows under Allen and Gerrard, with Rangers making signings who would become stalwarts of Gerrard's tenure, including Allan McGregor, Scott Arfield, Connor Goldson, Steven Davis, Glen Kamara and Ryan Kent.

When Rangers first announced they would be looking for a director of football in 2017, Ross Wilson's name was mentioned countless times as a leading candidate. Then Southampton's director of football operations, Wilson elected to stay on the south coast but would eventually be enticed north to Glasgow in October 2019. As Allen's replacement, he was tasked with taking the football department on to the next level and, in particular, developing the club's player trading model as one of his primary focuses.

'Nobody is more important at this club than the manager, the players and the chairman and investors, and Steven [Gerrard] has to be that front person,' said Wilson in a 2021 90min.com interview.

'Everything we have wanted to do we have progressed on. The exciting squad, developing our people, and the football infrastructure has been an exciting challenge. Steven and I go on record praising Douglas Park and investors, as we couldn't do it without them. The club has needed a lot of investment to get to where we have taken it to.

'Steven and I apply a lot of energy to this and we take it as a personal challenge to make the club as successful as we can. On his appointment, Steven surrounded himself with some excellent operators who all make a big contribution every day. It's a strong team we have – Gary McAllister, Michael Beale, Tom Culshaw, Colin Stewart, Jordan Milsom and Scott Mason.'

Wilson effectively utilised his contacts book and Rangers' scouting network over the three transfer windows between his appointment and the club securing the league title in May 2021. Players such as Ianis Hagi, Kemar Roofe and Leon Balogun arrived to furnish the club with the quality needed in key areas to progress to the next level.

'When I first sat down with Rangers to speak about this role, I made it abundantly clear that it was important I got the right staff and team around me. It's never about one person, it's always a collective effort and it's about finding the right people with the right skillset who can all bring their A game to the table and support the first team and academy players we're bringing through to make the team successful,' he explained.

Everything about Gerrard's Rangers was geared towards the collective. From support staff to the backroom team through to the first 11 who made their way on to the pitch, the feeling that this title-winning team was more significant than the sum of its parts was never far away from your thoughts. This doesn't happen by chance; it results from hours and hours of unseen work at the training centre both on and off the pitch to cultivate this environment that was the bedrock of the club's success.

Gary McAllister – Assistant Manager

As team-mates in Liverpool's midfield engine room, Gerrard and Rangers assistant manager Gary McAllister formed a close bond – despite the age differences – which has lasted for more than 20 years.

Upon the expiration of his Liverpool contract in the summer of 2002, McAllister joined Coventry City as player-manager.

He said he found the experience very difficult, such were the competing priorities of the two roles, the exacting demands on the modern-day manager and the financial difficulties the club were going through at the time.

In 2008, McAllister re-joined Leeds United as manager during their three-year spell in the third tier of English football. Despite a promising start, McAllister was relieved of his duties after just 11 months in charge in December 2008. Following a brief spell as first-team coach at Middlesbrough, he was enticed to Aston Villa as Gérard Houllier's assistant manager for a short period in 2010/11.

When Gerrard returned to Liverpool as a youth coach in early 2017, McAllister was also back at the club, having re-joined in July 2015 initially as first-team coach under Brendan Rodgers, but had then taken up an ambassadorial role following Rodgers' departure.

Despite McAllister only holding one coaching post in the previous few years, it appeared there was only one man Gerrard considered the perfect fit for his right-hand man when he was appointed at Ibrox in May 2018.

When speaking about selecting the staff who he wanted to take to Rangers, Gerrard told the club website:

'It was a very young group and inexperienced in terms of coaching [at first team level] so we needed an older head, someone who had been there and done it and knew the Scottish league inside out. Someone who could help us connect to Rangers very quickly.'

As assistant manager, McAllister was the conduit between the players and coaching staff. However, as you would expect, he was still more than active on the training pitch itself, mainly working with the midfielders. He could relate to the players and provide them with significant levels of insight from his playing career on either side of the border.

As the elder statesman of the group, McAllister brought a wealth of good experience to the team.

Across his playing career at Liverpool and Leeds (both as a player and manager) and his coaching career, McAllister mentions a few key values which have been fundamental through all those successful teams. Togetherness, clarity of messaging and absolute trust in the style of play through all challenges are all critical pillars of Gerrard's philosophy, and the coaching staff embodied this also.

Tom Culshaw – Technical Coach

Tom Culshaw and Gerrard are childhood friends from their days on Ironside Road in Huyton and played together in the same youth teams from the age of ten before joining the Liverpool academy. Culshaw's grandparents lived on the street, as did Gerrard's family, and their connection was mirrored throughout the generations, with their grandfathers and fathers also being close friends.

Culshaw came through the Liverpool academy with Gerrard and has remained close to him for many years, despite his early promise as a footballer failing to materialise into a playing career. Despite captaining the youth teams and playing for England Schoolboys around the same time as Jamie Carragher and Michael Owen, Culshaw was released by Liverpool at the age of 21.

On leaving the club, Culshaw told liverpool.com, 'When I left I found it tough going on trials for lower-league clubs. I got offered a couple of contracts at League Two clubs and I decided to knock them back thinking I could do a bit better.

'But when I started to go for trials it was taking longer and longer and then eventually, I just fell out of love with the game.

'My friend had a tarmacking firm, so I went and worked with all my mates for a while. It was hard. It was a tough few years for me. Especially when I saw my mates, the likes of Steven, Carra, Michael Owen – lads who I'd come through the youth team with – progressing. I probably had my first bump in the road at 21 and I just really didn't know how to handle it.'

After several years, Culshaw eventually rediscovered his love for the game during a spell abroad coaching young children and returned home to Liverpool, where he began to study and coach part-time at the Reds' academy.

Upon Gerrard's return to Liverpool, the two reunited as manager and coach of Liverpool's under-18s and Gerrard had this to say about his friend, 'When I started out full-time as an apprentice, Tommy was a year above me so I know everything about him and he knows everything about me.'

The two appear to display a balance of how life as a young footballer can go, with Gerrard becoming Liverpool and England captain. On the other hand, Culshaw elected to leave the professional game at 21 and try his hand at different things before being enticed back into coaching at a time he felt ready to impart his experience and knowledge to others.

When speaking about Culshaw's impact as a coach at Rangers, Gerrard said, 'Our defensive shape and organisation was a big priority in pre-season. Tom Culshaw would be scratching his head if I try to take the credit because he's the one who does a lot of unit work, and individual work with them.'

While each coach will be involved in all training areas, Culshaw is primarily known to many fans as the man responsible for the considerable improvement in Rangers' set pieces throughout his time at the club. Indeed, of the last 11 goals scored against arch-rivals Celtic at the time of writing this book, five came either from a corner or a free kick opportunity, which is in part down to the defensive work they put in on the training pitch, an area where Culshaw took an active role. The unerring focus on improving these areas of marginal gains was a key driver of Rangers' return to the top of Scottish football.

Michael Beale – First-Team Coach

'It would take me 15 to 20 years to get as good as Michael Beale as an on-pitch coach, to deliver sessions on a daily basis, so I let

Mick be Mick Beale because he's the expert and has the skillset,' Gerrard told Robbie Fowler's podcast.

This is what made Gerrard as a Rangers manager. He recognises that he cannot be all things to all people in the modern game and has surrounded himself with a team with the technical and man-management skills to deliver the football vision he has laid out. A club like Rangers – never more so than in May 2018 – requires a leader to act as the main public face and drag it forward to success.

Michael Beale was first team coach and was widely acknowledged as the brains behind Rangers' tactical philosophy and style of play. As with all members of the coaching team, he is keen to promote the benefit of the collective, but given the nature of this book, it's only natural that the focus throughout will be on that philosophy and style of which he was undoubtedly one of the key influences.

Beale's path to coaching at Rangers was reasonably unconventional, even in this era of successful managers who had less than illustrious playing careers. After coming through the Charlton youth academy at the same time as Paul Konchesky and Jermain Defoe, Beale quit professional football at the age of 21.

'I was a bit of a maverick. A left-winger – like a really bad Chris Waddle. I had the haircut and everything. I was a good dribbler and had a good left foot, but I wasn't great in the air for a tall kid and my right foot needed work,' he told thecoachesvoice.com

'When you're a good young player coming through, you tend to get a lot of pats on the back. But I needed more clarity from my coaches. Maybe it wasn't their fault – at that age, I was very muted, and I couldn't articulate what I needed.

'I was 21 when I left football – frustrated that it hadn't gone the way I wanted it to, and with my confidence at rock bottom. When I went into coaching, I was determined never to let a kid feel how I felt at the end. I was always going to talk to them about the full package.'

From there, Beale invested in a Brazilian Soccer Schools franchise to teach futsal to kids in London. This resulted in him doing enough to earn a part-time coaching role at his boyhood club Chelsea in 2001. Beale progressed through the ranks at Stamford Bridge, culminating in a full-time job at Chelsea's academy working with the under-14 squad.

'My wife thought I was joking when I came home from work one day and said I was leaving Chelsea to go to Liverpool. It meant taking a big pay cut and moving home. All when we'd just had a baby – our first boy, Henry. But I needed change. A new challenge.

'At Chelsea, I felt we had the best players, so we all won. Every coach won. I'd started asking myself – were we winning, or were the players winning for us? I needed to explore that.'

The move to Liverpool in 2012 would see him take charge of the under-16 squad primarily and assist Alex Inglethorpe, now Liverpool's academy manager, with the under-23s. Beale would eventually be appointed in this role full-time during a hugely successful period where 18 academy players would make their first-team debuts, including Trent Alexander-Arnold.

Brazilian goalkeeping legend Rogério Ceni retired from playing in 2015, and while on a year-long sabbatical in Europe, he took the opportunity to study for his coaching badges. As part of this trip, Ceni had arranged to meet with other coaches to discuss the game and share ideas. As one of the top youth coaches in the country at the time, Beale was recommended to Ceni, and the Brazilian came to Liverpool's training centre to oversee a session with Liverpool under-23s where the two men discussed in depth their footballing philosophies. Almost immediately after travelling home to Brazil, Ceni was offered the head coach job at São Paulo in early 2017, and he wasted no time picking up the phone to offer Beale a role as his assistant.

Beale described his time in Brazil as a huge learning experience. Given this was his first role working with a first team, he introduced more tactical concepts to the players than would ordinarily be found in academy football. This was the bridge between his love of developing young footballers and his love of tactics which we would see working together perfectly at Rangers. Unfortunately, his time in Brazil was short as Beale chose to resign after seven months with the financial realities of Brazilian football proving challenging.

'Initially, things went fantastically well at São Paulo. I think we lost one in the first 20 games, and the training and day-to-day life was a dream. Unfortunately, in Brazilian football, finances are often an issue – and our club was in debt.

'Nine of our starting team were sold and, just like that, the project changed. I found that really difficult because I was used to building; to developing. When our team kept changing, I realised it wasn't going to be a long-term project.

'In the end, I was there for seven months. But it was seven months of learning every single day. Seven months of developing into a more confident coach.'

Beale returned to a senior academy post at Liverpool – where Gerrard was now heading up the under-18 development squad – and continued studying for his UEFA Pro Licence. Still, the desire to get back into senior football was never far from his mind. Despite not working together during their time at Liverpool, Beale was made aware that Gerrard was considering him for the role of first-team coach at Rangers, something he immediately disregarded as nonsense until the call came, and he headed north to Glasgow.

Scott Mason – Head of Data Analysis

Scott Mason led the data analysis team at Rangers, and his team focused primarily on post-match and opposition analysis. As with the rest of the coaching staff, Scott had also worked at Liverpool, in various performance analysis roles since 2012. When Gerrard returned to Liverpool as a coach, he appointed Scott as a performance analyst and worked with him throughout that year. Scott was a late addition to the Rangers team, joining one year later than the rest of the staff in summer 2019. Speaking on *Relentle55: The Inside Story*, Gerrard had this to say when discussing building the analysis department when he joined the club:

'That's took time from an analysis point of view. I tried to get Scott in year one, but unfortunately, the timing wasn't right; he joined us at a later date, and he's been phenomenal in his role, supported by Graeme [Stevenson] and Seb [Dunn] in that department.'

Data analysis is relatively new within football, certainly compared to other sports. In American sports, gleaning every last scrap of insight from data is nothing new and has been a regular feature for many years. Anyone familiar with the term 'moneyball' will have an understanding of the benefits that can come with integrating data and insights into your club that can bring. The breadth of data that can be collected on players and teams is ever-growing, from basic metrics such as the number of passes made in a game to detailed health and fitness information used to prevent injuries. As with most situations, knowledge is power. Understanding this data and using it in a way that can benefit your team is a vastly sought-after skill within the modern game.

At Rangers, the analysis team work closely with the coaching staff and will primarily be tasked with creating video clips and preparing high-level insights from previous games. The coaches can then use these to reinforce or introduce key learning for individual team members or the entire squad to take into future games.

Speaking to Rangers TV, Mason gave an insight into the analysis team during his time at Rangers and how they integrated with the wider footballing staff, 'There are three of us within the department. There's myself, Graeme and Seb who has come on board not long ago.

'In terms of my role and what I do, I look after the post-match analysis. So after the game, I'll go through and look at where we were strong and look at where we can possibly improve.

'I'll then feed that back to the coaches and also look at how it impacts upon our philosophy and how our style of play is dictated to within that game.

'Also within that, we are trying to look at the improvement of individual players. So through conversations or trends I see along maybe three or four games, how can I put forward the clips or support the players in suggesting ways in which they can improve, or just highlight areas in which they are doing really well.'

While the focus of performance analysis is analysing what happened in the previous game, it is always with an eye on how the team can improve in the next match, as Mason outlines further, 'It is a joint effort leading into the next game. I will debrief what we have done in the previous game and pick out anything I feel is relevant.

'Graeme will do the pre-match analysis, so he will have a look at the strengths and weaknesses of the opposition.

'Then there will maybe be one or two bits the coaching staff would like to add as well. So with all of that, we try to bring it all together within a meeting.

'It is a collaborative effort. I might add a bit from my end, Graeme his side and also then the coaching staff in order to give the players a game plan that we think will work for that game.'

Setting the Tactical Vision

'A vision on football is not a formation. It is your preferences for style of play in attack, defence and the moments of transition in between. It also includes the behaviours, standards and culture you would like to create inside the club,' said Michael Beale.

Three key areas underpinned Beale's vision for Rangers. Principles, people, system. The system was the visual embodiment of the hard work underneath to develop a style of play, recruit the right people and implement the correct values at the club.

From the cohesive, well-drilled Rangers starting 11 we saw on the pitch twice a week, it became abundantly clear the value Steven Gerrard placed on the importance of the collective. The wider staff can be overlooked in football as they are not always as front and centre as the players and managers are. Still, there are many more layers to building a successful team than simply putting the right players in the correct positions and asking them to play.

Gerrard set the footballing vision at Rangers and then trusted his coaching staff and the players to implement this on his behalf as Beale told The Coaches Voice.

'We have a culture and a set of non-negotiables that everyone lives by. In my head, I want to play a certain way, and I want to be a really tough team to play against, a really aggressive team. We move around the pitch together and own the pitch.

'You want to play in a style that entertains the fans. You score goals and be creative, and that's how you see it in your head.

'But what happens if you are playing a team like Porto or Benfica who've got more expensive players than you, players with more experience? Teams who, maybe player for player, are operating on a different level from you?

'I can't approach that game the way I would a game at home against a team who are at the bottom of the league. So it's about being able to adapt from game to game.'

If you spend time listening to how Gerrard wants to play, a few key messages will always come to the fore. He wants his teams first and foremost to be compact, organised and tough to play against when out of possession. When Rangers had the ball, the expectation was that the team will move around the pitch together as a unit and play a possession-based style to attack opponents and score as many goals as possible.

Aside from this being his first managerial job, some keen observers were wondering whether Gerrard's philosophy would in any way mirror his playing style. He was revered for his all-action displays and capable of performing all over the park, but less so for his positional or tactical awareness.

He is a manager who is aware of his strengths, and that's why he approached Beale to come in as first-team coach, having been impressed by his methods and reputation during their time as academy coaches at Liverpool. Beale was responsible for most of the training sessions day to day, including the tactical work on the training pitch. At the same time, Gerrard preferred to oversee and ensure standards were set. As such, the principles outlined here are a collective tactical approach by the Rangers staff with Gerrard as the leader-manager.

Coming into a new club, it's vital to gain immediate awareness of the club's size, history, standing in their domestic league, and supporters' expectations.

'You arrive at a club with a history and you arrive in a moment. Unless you're very fortunate, you're likely to arrive at a club who's not been doing so well,' said Beale.

This was the case when Gerrard and his team joined Rangers. They arrived at a big club with an illustrious history and a huge fanbase. But it was also a club in disarray on the pitch, still grappling with the expectations of those fans who yearned for glory days of years gone by.

The importance, therefore, of setting a clear vision for how Gerrard wanted this Rangers team to play was crucial in those early days of the pre-season in June 2018. Given the coaching experience and background of the coaching team, it will come as no surprise how heavily influenced their collective vision is from their time spent working in youth development in England.

At Rangers, the game model must be influenced by the club's history and position as the most successful in Scottish football. To that end, some clear principles aligned to the vision become quickly apparent. Both Beale and Gerrard are on record as saying they favour high-energy, attacking football fans want to see, and players want to play. Therefore, Rangers would be dominant in possession, play aggressive, expansive football with intensity, and always try to maintain a solid defensive base. Given the disparity between the teams faced domestically and in Europe, a strong theme of flexibility and adaptability was also required to run through the vision. This allowed the team to have an element of unpredictability heading into each game.

While the team had a solid, well-coached defensive structure, this element of unpredictability evolved in several areas of the pitch. In possession, Rangers nominally lined up in a 4-3-2-1 shape with one deeper-lying midfielder and two attacking full-backs. When facing particular challenges, however, the team also retained the flexibility to drop a second midfielder deeper to form a double pivot or vary the positioning of one or both full-backs as situations demanded.

In the attacking areas, as the seasons progressed, Rangers also introduced flexibility with tweaks to individual roles of the wider midfielders and forwards, the selection of players with different skillsets and changes to the formation in specific game scenarios.

The vision at Rangers under Gerrard was notably based on the players and their individual qualities, which made this unique to Rangers. The club adopted a 'You vs Yourself' mentality as part of their player development plan, something they saw as the journey a player undertakes throughout the early stages of his career. The key idea within this is for each player to constantly look to improve themselves every day, whether through training or playing matches. To realise this, Rangers also had to create an elite training environment within which the players had the freedom to flourish.

'I was obsessed,' Gerrard told thisisanfield.com. 'Obsessed with being the best player in training every single day, and if I didn't, I'd go home and think about it and try and do it again the next day.

'You have to be obsessed. When you get that sniff and that little bit of hope, you've got to be obsessed to move team-mates out of the way. Once you're in, they're not coming back.'

When asked about talented players who aren't obsessed, Gerrard added, 'The word "talent" frustrates me. I love talent, and I love seeing it, but at Liverpool's academy, the important thing is they need to understand the other side of the game. Fighting, winning, tackling and going where it hurts, letting your lungs burns, really digging deep.

'When kids want to give up, you can't do that at Premier League and Champions League level.

'Just as important as talent is the other side of the game.'

Setting a vision is not just about player development or the tactical philosophy. Gerrard, Beale and sporting director Ross Wilson often spoke about how vital recruitment was to Rangers in those early months. The bedrocks of the 55th title were either already at the club – in the cases of James Tavernier, Ryan Jack and Alfredo Morelos – or would join in that first summer transfer window, such as Allan McGregor, Connor

Goldson, Steven Davis, Glen Kamara, Scott Arfield and Ryan Kent. Recruiting talented players is essential, but so is recruiting the correct type of characters and mentality who you can be confident will lead inside the dressing room on your behalf.

That continual investment in new players who fully align to the club's vision was a huge factor in Rangers' incremental improvement throughout the three years leading up to being crowned champions once more.

The setting of the vision is far from a once and done scenario. It is constantly reviewed and iterated with the whole staff tasked with promoting the concept at every opportunity to help control the narrative. The key to the success of the vision is an unequivocal alignment throughout the club, from the senior executives on the board to the management team, backroom staff and the playing squad.

On the pitch, four fundamental tenets came through repeatedly when you listen to both Gerrard and Beale speak. They are own the pitch, own the ball, win in both penalty boxes, and the importance of mentality and character.

Out of Possession – Own the Pitch

Defensive organisation is not sexy, but it is a crucial component of any successful side. It stands to reason that if you are a team with a solid defensive unit, you can control games more from deep and expect to have more possession of the ball. A well-structured defensive shape results in having to expend less energy when pressing the opposition, allowing Rangers to play with 'less stress' as Michael Beale puts it and be better prepared to attack when possession is recovered. This resulted in a defensive shape that never feels overly exposed or has players sprinting to get into position while the opponent attempts to attack.

Generally, Rangers elected to set up a hybrid 4-3-2-1 formation that proved incredibly successful over Gerrard's first three years in charge. Teams such as Villarreal, Midtjylland, Feyenoord, Porto, Braga, Galatasaray, Standard Liege and Benfica experienced frustrating evenings when attempting to penetrate this Rangers team. Throughout the three years up to May 2021, Rangers played 45 Europa League fixtures, losing only six. In just two of those defeats – 3-1 to Leverkusen at Ibrox in March 2020 and 2-0 to Slavia Prague – Rangers lost by more than one goal.

The time and effort invested in the defensive structure was apparent from the very first games under Gerrard. Solid performances came against Aberdeen when down to ten men early in the first half during his first SPFL game and the backs-to-the-wall nine-man victory against FC Ufa to qualify for the Europa League group stages just a few weeks later.

There are several key principles the coaching staff considered when deciding on their defensive approach for each game. The overall philosophy was set and would not change, but the game model itself needed to be flexible given the differing quality of opposition they would face game to game.

For example, the defensive line would be positioned much higher in domestic games where Rangers could expect to control 60 per cent of possession and play most of the match in the opposition's half. Similarly, Rangers would be expected to be less aggressive out of possession in European games, particularly away from Ibrox, as breaking from their defensive shape would provide high-quality teams with the opportunity to counter-attack.

Narrow and Compact Defensive Shape

As you can see from the image on the opposite page, Rangers' much vaunted defensive shape was commonly comprised of two central defenders and three central midfielders.

Figure 1

They were instructed to remain narrow and compact and form a 'five' with the stated aims of defending versus the ball and protecting the centre of the defensive red zone. That's not to say that these players would play exclusively in deep defensive areas, as doing so would be counter-intuitive to their high-energy attacking mantra. It would also enable the opposition to occupy more advanced areas of the pitch in more significant numbers, thus increasing their opportunities to attack.

This strong defensive shape allowed both full-backs to act as de facto wingers throughout Gerrard's tenure, which reaped significant rewards, but the work of the two wider central midfielders who provided lateral cover for their full-backs was one of the cornerstones of the team's defensive prowess.

The coaching staff also placed great emphasis on how important it is to occupy the entire width of the pitch when

NARROW & COMPACT DEFENSIVE SHAPE

LEFT WING   HALF-SPACE   CENTRUM   HALF-SPACE   RIGHT WING

Rangers' 'two and three' defensive shape allowed the team to remain compact in central areas and reduce the risk of the opposition creating high quality chances.

FIGURE 1

planning a tactical structure and always to be looking to find depth on the pitch. They reasoned that your opponent will always be able to reduce the depth of the pitch – whether that be literally using different pitch dimensions – or by employing a higher defensive line and implementing an offside strategy. The one thing they cannot alter is the width in which your team can play.

The principal aim of Rangers' defensive strategy was to block the centre of the pitch to keep the ball away from this area, as this is where the highest concentration of quality chances are taken. Rangers would therefore attempt to force the opposition out wide for the very same reason. The percentage of crosses that result in goals is a lot lower than that of shots taken centrally. In certain situations – such as the Europa League group stage in 2020/21 – Rangers conceded a significant proportion of goals as a result of these situations, and while much is made of how susceptible Rangers are to attacks in behind their full-backs, this was an accepted risk within the overall tactical structure of the team.

At times, the defensive approach could be tailored to specific challenges such as one or both full-backs playing slightly withdrawn roles in certain games to counter against an opposition change of shape, or the placing of a second striker in the forward line to help block opposition passing through the lines.

Rangers were well placed to enact their own pressing strategy in the midfield battlegrounds by forcing opposition players deeper and wider when they were in possession.

Do the Maths

'The pitch is the same size for both teams. Your team must understand how to use the space better than your opponents.'

Doing the maths is another concept that Michael Beale liked to utilise in Rangers' defensive set-up and this was built around some easily identifiable assumptions. Based on an opponent's position on the park, Rangers assumed that the least dangerous players in the opposition team would be positioned furthest away from their goal (i.e. the goalkeeper and centre-backs). Therefore, their pressing strategy was tailored to ensuring those players saw the bulk of possession and did so in the opposition defensive third.

Conversely, Rangers would analyse which opposition players posed the most significant threat and devised strategies to ensure their time on the ball was limited. If they did receive the ball, Rangers aimed to have the proportional defensive cover or try to push the player wider on the pitch to minimise impact to the centre of their own 18-yard box.

How Rangers approached each game aligned with the club's overall vision and view of themselves compared to each opposition. If Rangers were playing away against a team like Benfica, they might elect to play in a lower block and allow Benfica's centre-backs possession in areas that were not dangerous. In theory, this gave Rangers a ten v eight defensive situation, as only eight outfield Benfica players are ahead of the ball. As soon as the centre-backs attempted to make a pass either to the full-backs or into the middle of the pitch, Rangers would look to press and try to regain possession of the ball.

Figure 2
Pressing Strategy

At its basic level, when a team presses the opposition, it is with the intent of closing down the player in possession of the ball with the sole focus of winning it back. There are various strategies and intensities with which teams press. Still, the success of this will mainly be determined by how the players tasked with pressing work together as a unit by blocking off the passing options and exposing weaknesses in the opposition team.

A team pressing strategy can be informed by a few key questions. Which type of opposition are you playing against? Is this a European game away from home against a high-quality

FORCE TEAMS WIDE

PASS/SHOT   PLAYER MOVEMENT

Rangers' solid central shape was designed with the aim of forcing teams wider into
less dangerous attacking areas.

FIGURE 2

team, or are you playing at home against a team you should expect to dominate possession comfortably against? How do you want to structure our press based on this? If a team comes to Ibrox to sit in and defend deep, it doesn't make any sense for Rangers to employ a low defensive block and try to entice teams out, as most times they are coming with the sole purpose to camp on the edge of their box and escape with what they can. The defensive shape when out of possession was directly linked to how Rangers wanted to attack depending on the opposition or game state. The game plan was flexible and designed in that way to ensure Rangers maximised their strengths and minimised their weaknesses.

There are many contrasting challenges any Rangers team faces on a weekly basis, whether it be against European opponents or closer to home. With that in mind, having the capability to 'adjust the dial' as Beale refers to it in order to vary their pressing intensity was a crucial skill for this team to have mastered.

In most games, Rangers' first line of defence would look to position themselves high when an opposition team is in possession in their back line. When playing against a four-man defence, the three forwards would position themselves between the player in possession and any nearby open team-mates. This technique is called 'cover shadow' and allows the attacking player to essentially cover more space than a basic man-marking strategy would allow.

In European games, the opposition are more likely to drop their centre-backs deeper to pick the ball up from the goalkeeper. Therefore, Rangers would look to keep their front three narrow to block passing lanes into the centre of the pitch.

When facing a three-man defence, Rangers usually positioned their full-backs higher in these situations to man-mark their opposite numbers, again with the intent of ensuring opposition teams were unable to quickly progress through the lines.

43

Any of these approaches required significant buy-in from the midfield three. They would be required to provide support of the forwards' press and shuttle out laterally in support of the full-backs should the opposition successfully play through. The responsibilities placed on the wider central midfielders cannot be underplayed or undervalued. Such is the crucial nature of this to the overall cohesion and balance of the team.

Figure 3

When we talk about pressing, we can break this down into three key areas of the pitch. You have the offensive pressing zone in the opponents' defensive third, the midfield pressing zone, and the defensive pressing zone in your defensive third. Each of these zones will – for the most part – align to the terms high press, mid-block, and low block.

Rangers under Steven Gerrard placed particular focus on using the mid-block in certain games. This was in part because regaining the ball in this area can lead to high-quality opportunities if the opposing team's defensive players are taken far enough away from their goal. Conversely, using a mid-block approach means Rangers were less susceptible to counter-attacks should opponents play their way through the lines of pressure. By playing in this way, Rangers could be relatively comfortable that their pressing strategy was flexible enough to cope with most in-game scenarios. Similarly, they were able to ensure that their central defenders were not positioned too high but instead would occupy areas of the pitch in which they were most comfortable.

Pressing in itself is intrinsically linked to the specific moments of each game, and players must know how the team want to attack beforehand and be aware when each should be adopted within the game. Pressing as a cohesive unit was fundamental for Rangers and required complete buy-in from the team collective. Again, the use of wide triangles and control of width was essential to Rangers' approach as by adopting a

RANGERS' PRESSING STRATEGY

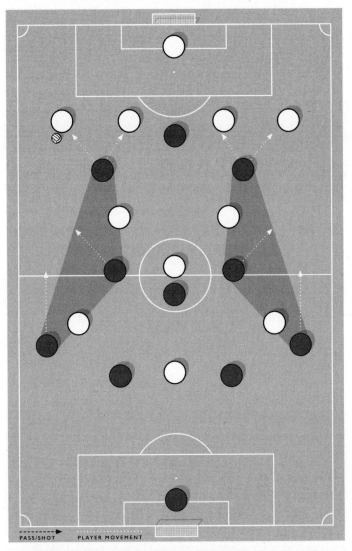

Rangers' use of wide triangles on either side of the pitch was a key tenet of their pressing strategy.
The full-back, ball-side central midfielder and ball-side number ten would form a unit out of possession with
the intent of limiting the opposition team's ability to attack.

FIGURE 3

strategy where the players began to press from central areas of the pitch and looked to run wider, sometimes known as a curved press, they could use the width of the pitch to their advantage. This allowed the team to box in opposition full-backs and wide players, thus reducing their passing options.

Should Rangers adopt a higher-intensity press against teams who come to Ibrox and sit deep to frustrate, they would look to apply a similar approach. The number tens would provide cover shadow to the opposition full-backs, and the central striker would block both centre-backs from progressing through the lines by positioning himself between them. This allowed Rangers' defenders to be flexible enough to deal with the opposition in defensive areas while also having appropriate cover to manage any overloads should the opposition pass through.

Rangers deliberately instruct their three forwards to stay high and only track back sporadically when out of possession with the deliberate intent of ensuring they are in a position to attack quickly should the ball be won back in deeper areas of the pitch. There is another element of risk here as the forwards could drop deeper to assist the full-backs from a defensive viewpoint. Still, by electing not to do that, Rangers can maintain an offensive threat even when defending their own box.

In the example next page, we see how Rangers' forwards used pressing triggers to apply pressure to Livingston's defence in the 2-0 victory in October 2020. As the ball was passed across the defensive line, Ryan Kent sprang to close down the recipient and attempt to regain possession in a dangerous area of the pitch and attack a three v three defensive situation. Kent successfully impacted the defender to the extent that Rangers regained possession through Jermain Defoe. The ball eventually broke to Ianis Hagi, who ran from deep to give Rangers more significant numbers in attack. This is a perfect example of how pressing weaker members of the opposition can lead to a very dangerous attacking situation and it culminated in Rangers scoring through Joe Aribo.

Figure 4

PRESSING TRIGGERS

Rangers 2 - 0 Livingston SPFL Ibrox Stadium 25.10.20

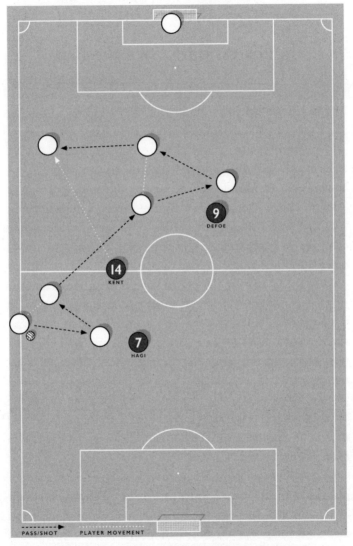

PASS/SHOT --------▶   PLAYER MOVEMENT

Rangers' use of pressing triggers when specific opposition players are in possession were a key feature of their overall pressing strategy.

FIGURE 4

In Possession – Own the Ball

Michael Beale believes, 'Utopia for me is finding a group of players that have freedom to rotate in the final third.'

When discussing possession in football, there is still a tendency to link this to how successful a team is, possibly a consequence of Barcelona's conquering tiki-taka approach of 2008 to 2012. All time spent on the ball is not equal, as we witnessed with Leicester's 2016 Premier League triumph, which came on the back of an average possession per game of just 43 per cent.

With the rise in popularity of pressing and counter-pressing, teams are more than happy to concede possession to the opposition in less threatening areas of the pitch and await their opportunities to spring forward and attack. Therefore, possession statistics do not tell the whole story. Ultimately stats such as goals and shots on target can be more effective measures when analysing how a team has performed in a game. Advanced statistics such as expected goals, which directly measures the quality of chances created by a team, can also reflect how a team has performed.

Particularly at Ibrox, Rangers will have the lion's share of possession in the vast majority of matches. With such a high amount of time spent on the ball, the importance of what you do with it becomes even more paramount.

Beale describes the time a team spends in possession as the nice part of football and will always try to base his style on having possession in the opposition's half regardless of any in-game scenarios. The reasons for this are numerous, but as always, the defensive focus is never too far away. Being in possession in the opposition half means you are further away from your own goal and therefore less likely to concede. As an opposite to the strategy when out of possession, the key aim for Rangers in possession under Steven Gerrard was to maximise the time attacking players spent in possession in dangerous areas of the pitch and minimise the time they had sterile possession deep in their own half.

Rangers instilled a process when the team have the ball, which Beale called a collective identity flow, a concept he has used since his days coaching kids in the Chelsea academy.

This flow focuses on three methods of attacking an opponent's defensive structure to identify and understand where spaces may appear within the opposition team's defensive structure for the team to attack. Can we attack centrally through their defensive lines? If not, can we get the ball to our wide players in dangerous areas with a view to going around their defensive block and creating crossing opportunities that way? Failing that, can we utilise our deeper players' passing range to create openings over the top of a team, whether that is long diagonal balls into channels or more directly into the penalty box?

Figure 5

'The formation you choose is not all that important. Whatever the on-paper formation, the players can form different shapes in-game, and the freedom to rotate is key to making this happen. The ability to be flexible and unpredictable is key in the modern game,' Beale told The Coches' Voice.

Throughout the first 12 months under Gerrard, it was widely documented that the team struggled intermittently with playing through ultra-defensive opponents. The work done on the training pitch to hone this approach and purchase players more suited to positional rotation and combination play in tight

FINDING SPACE TO ATTACK

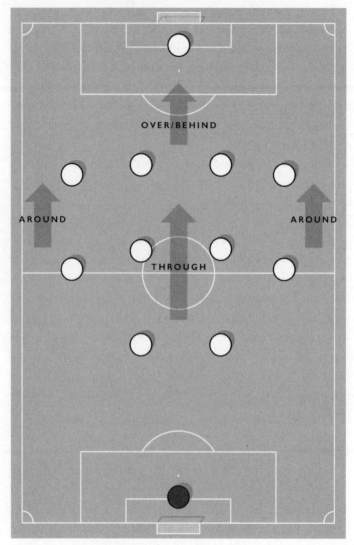

The different approaches a team can take when attacking.

FIGURE 5

central areas was a critical factor in becoming champions. With such a high level of positional flexibility, it's clear to see why Beale believes formations are not the be all and end all when discussing football tactics. That being said, the coaching team did elect to switch from a 4-3-3 formation in March 2019 to a 4-3-2-1 by asking the wide players to play narrower on the pitch and closer to the central striker.

The coaching staff put a considerable focus on how to overload in attack to continually upset opposition defensive lines. This is implemented using the players' inherent flexibility.

As Rangers progressed through the three seasons under Gerrard, the shape in possession became less of a 4-3-2-1 and more of an ultra-attacking 2-3-4-1 in most domestic games. The full-backs were positioned so high, they became in essence the fourth and fifth members of the forward line and were ably supported by the strong defensive base behind.

Figure 6

Leon Balogun and Filip Helander were both centre-backs who predominantly played on the left of central defence for Rangers; however, their playing styles and skillsets are polar opposites. Balogun preferred to play higher and carry the ball out of defence into midfield while relying on his superior recovery pace, whereas Helander was much more of a classic centre-back who viewed his main job as defending and would use his anticipation and positioning skills to impressive effect. A flexible, experienced team therefore can change how they defend and also how they attack with the addition of just one player to the line-up. Joe Aribo and Scott Arfield shared the right-sided centre-midfield role in 2020/21. The former excelled with the ball at his feet, where he was able to showcase his incredible close control and dribbling skills. In contrast, Arfield had a laser focus on impacting the final third of the pitch, concentrating on getting beyond the strikers to cause maximum damage to the opposition. Where the space is on

2-3-4-1 FORMATION IN POSSESSION

Rangers' attacking shape in possession more closely resembled a 2-3-4-1 formation.

FIGURE 6

the pitch changes many times throughout the course of a game, so every single practice in training should be geared towards understanding where this space can be at any fixed moment and which player is best placed to take advantage of it.

At Rangers, the only outfield players who did not engage in some form of positional rotation were the two centre-backs. Their role was key in building out from the back, but who they passed the ball to would primarily be dependent on the moment of the game. There was a level of freedom for the rest of the team that allowed them to move around the pitch in that search for depth. There were several key relationships within the team that would enable this almost telepathic understanding to take place.

Figure 7
Occupying Width and Searching for Depth
As mentioned in the 'Own the Pitch' section, the ability to occupy width and search for depth can be used in both the defensive and offensive phases of play.

By occupying the width and ensuring you have an appropriate spread of players in each vertical zone of the pitch, you will get greater success due to the variation of player positions when using rotations and combination play to break down teams. Again, Beale came back to his feelings that formations can be less relevant if you can put the hours in on the training pitch to implement these concepts and gain meaningful possession in crucial attacking areas.

Relationships on the pitch were key to Rangers' tactical philosophy and come back to that principles, people, system approach. 'Are we playing together or just at the same time?' is a mantra that's also oft-repeated by Beale in the many webinars and podcasts he has guested on. Putting players on a pitch together does not make you play well together as a team. In any walk of life – but particularly in sport – teamwork is the key to success. Developing together as a team and forming

POSITIONAL ROTATION

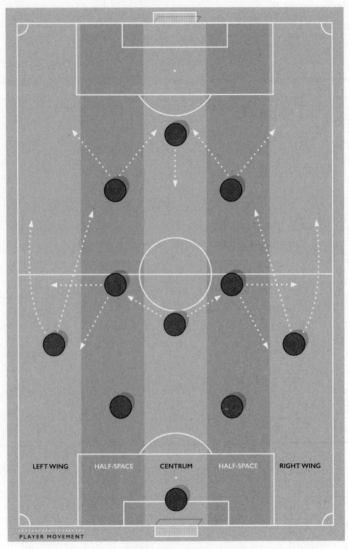

Rangers' use of positional rotation was key to meeting their aims of finding space by occupying width and searching for depth.

FIGURE 7

close bonds will significantly improve the team's cohesion and efficiency.

As shown previously when discussing Rangers' pressing approach, the full-back, wide central midfielder and wide attacker on both flanks also played a crucial role when Rangers were in possession of the ball. All three regularly rotated positions when the circumstances required it. It was a similar story with the midfield three and front three, where each unit of the team would interchange fluidly throughout each game.

In midfield, Steven Davis would nominally sit deeper with the two central midfielders being free to attack vertically. In attack, Ryan Kent may drop into the traditional number ten role and allow the two remaining forwards to work as a more conventional two-man strike force should the situation have demanded it.

Rangers tended to build up in possession in several different ways.

Connor Goldson's distribution, in particular, was crucial as he could create those opportunities with a variety of line-breaking passes through midfield directly into the opposition defensive third. Goldson also retained the capability to either build play down the right or draw the opposition defensive shape over to that side of the pitch, then quickly play a long diagonal switch of play over to the left-back and try to take advantage of an overload.

Should Rangers build from deep, both full-backs would place themselves high in their own half, safe in the knowledge that the two wider central midfielders could provide lateral cover should possession be lost. Against teams defending in a low block, Rangers also often utilised long passes from Allan McGregor to the head of James Tavernier to break the opposition line of pressure and build down the right flank.

Another option for Rangers during build-up play was to use Tavernier as an inverted full-back to make good use of his running power and ability on the ball in the half-space. In these situations, the wide central midfielder and wide attacker would look to stretch play laterally to allow him to advance forward inside the pitch when in possession of the ball. Like Liverpool under Klopp, the Rangers midfield three could be described as more functional than creative, although this has evolved throughout the three years of Gerrard, particularly in this title-winning campaign. Prior to this, it was rare to see incisive or direct passes from the centre of the pitch. The primary objective of the midfield unit was to retain possession and initiate runs and rotations from the full-backs and attackers.

Figure 8

Depending on the opposition and game state at the time, this slow build-up play can be used as a tactic to draw opposition defenders out of shape to allow us to utilise those attacking players in more space.

Outplaying Your Direct Opponent

'It's no secret that a team full of players that are happy to play in the one vs one moments are often the most successful and that this is the purest form of the game,' explained Michael Beale on his coaching website.

Players who have the ability to outplay one on one and eliminate direct opponents are vital in the final third of the pitch. When space is limited in the opposition defensive third, having attacking players who are strong when facing up to defenders one on one and capable of beating them in several different ways, whether through dribbling, one-touch play or pace, is crucial. Flexibility in attack is encouraged through positional rotations and fast, incisive combination play on the flanks.

When speaking to the *Heart and Hand* podcast in an interview in May 2019, Beale again underlined the importance of recruiting players who could excel in one vs one situations, whether that be the way that Glen Kamara is able to receive

RANGERS' FLEXIBLE BUILD-UP

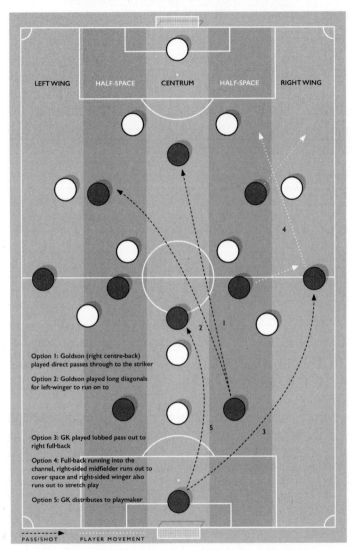

LEFT WING   HALF-SPACE   CENTRUM   HALF-SPACE   RIGHT WING

Option 1: Goldson (right centre-back)
played direct passes through to the striker

Option 2: Goldson played long diagonals
for left-winger to run on to

Option 3: GK played lobbed pass out to
right full-back

Option 4: Full-back running into the
channel, right-sided midfielder runs out to
cover space and right-sided winger also
runs out to stretch play

Option 5: GK distributes to playmaker

PASS/SHOT   PLAYER MOVEMENT

Rangers utilised several different approaches to progress the ball when attacking.

FIGURE 8

the ball under pressure and use his 'Action Man hips' to swivel away from markers, or Ryan Kent in a more traditional manner by being able to take the ball past players on either side using his pace and dribbling ability.

The benefits of adding players who can receive the ball on the half-turn and are strong one on one are numerous, but in Rangers' case, this was often used to draw defensive pressure to these players and allow others who excel off the ball to find space and expose gaps in tight defences.

Tempo and Counter Pressing

Tempo is defined as the rate or speed of a motion or activity, and in sport, this can translate to how quickly a team is moving the ball in the attacking phase of play.

Consistently and effectively playing with a high tempo in a possession-based philosophy while trying to play one-touch football is a difficult thing to achieve for all but the elite teams. To do this consistently is the result of many months and years on the training pitch to learn repetitions and gain almost telepathic understanding with your team-mates. To that end, most teams aim to play two-touch football, with one touch to receive the pass and the other to circulate the ball.

Beale talked about the ability to 'turn the dial', which was also true with regard to tempo. In essence, tempo can be used as a counter-pressing strategy as well as in the attacking phase of play.

In certain scenarios, Rangers would look to deliberately play with that slower tempo as a means of assessing the opposition's pressing approach and encourage teams to break their structure and allow Rangers to overload certain areas as and when they see fit. A good example of this would be the slow build-up play Rangers utilised on the right-hand side of the park, but then quickly switching play over to the left to find Borna Barišić in space to attack in a dangerous area. Using a shorter passing approach rather than constantly searching for long balls over the top, encouraged Rangers' attackers to rotate positions more and drop deep to create gaps in the opposition structure and in turn become harder to mark.

When we think of pressing in British football, our mind is drawn back to that Liverpool connection and their manager, Jürgen Klopp. From his time in charge of Mainz and Borussia Dortmund, the German's tactical style became known as 'gegenpressing', which translates to counter-pressing in English. This is a term that has been around for many years. Many successful teams have adopted pressing and counter-pressing strategies throughout history, from the Total Football of the Netherlands in the 1970s to Arrigo Sacchi's outstanding Milan teams of the late '80s and early '90s.

But it was not widely known or implemented and certainly not to the scale we see now. In years gone by, when a team lost possession of the ball in attacking areas, it was natural for them to drop deep into their defensive shape to protect their goal from an expected counter-attack. Counter-pressing can be used as a means to simply win the ball back and retain possession following a turnover. This was something that Pep Guardiola's team excelled at; however, there are further layers and benefits which Klopp's teams began to explore.

While winning the ball back will never not be beneficial, there is a generally accepted school of thought that a team is at their weakest immediately after they have regained possession in their own half. They will be set in a defensive tactical structure, whereas the attacking team is still positioned in their attacking structure. Therefore, as the defensive team look to reorganise themselves to commit men forward on the counter with the intention of catching the opposition off guard, gaps will appear in their shape, which attacking players are well placed to take advantage of. To that end, the team who have just lost possession of the ball will immediately press the opposition in their own defensive areas with the intent to block their passing lanes, look to reclaim the ball and launch an attack of their own.

With Rangers adding more players in later seasons who were more attack-minded and capable of dribbling with the ball, this also had a positive impact on the team's counter-pressing strategy. These players would constantly look to create space using off-ball movements and expose gaps in defensive blocks, but with the solid midfield structure behind them it meant that should possession of the ball be lost, the line of players behind were able to effectively squeeze the space underneath and position themselves perfectly to counter-press the opposition.

Mentality and Character

Good coaching and management doesn't start and end solely on the training pitch. Football players are complex, with many different personalities and outlooks on life; therefore, managing the person and the player is key to any future success. The idea of developing a player mentality has followed Michael Beale throughout his coaching career, and he told The Coaches' Voice about the mentality required to progress yourself as a person and footballer:

'Players who are engaged, challenged, supported and provoked in training every day will respond to their coach. They will also have greater belief in the project they are part of.'

Under the principles, people and system mantra that Gerrard and Beale adopt, the value placed in developing young players mentally runs through the entire ethos. There is a belief that you manage the person first, then you look to develop the player and eventually, this will organically improve the team.

When you consider the type of players who joined Rangers in those three full seasons, they were all signed at different stages in their own journeys and careers. Players were plucked from elite academy environments using the cross-border loophole, they came from the top five European leagues and also several players made the switch from playing domestically against Rangers in the Scottish top flight. Understanding a player's journey to arrive at your club is key to assisting them in developing technical skills and mentality.

This process is key to aid the overall development of both young players and a football club, as Beale outlined on the *Training Guru* podcast:

'What you find with a lot of successful people is that communication and clarity are huge, and they have that personality to inspire, to get under people's skin, to get them to believe in a vision.

'The best coaches in the world have the ability to keep people on that "you versus yourself" journey and sell an exciting vision. That's the one thing I would say about all the coaches I've seen, be it Jürgen Klopp, Brendan Rodgers, that ability to inspire people with your personality and vision, and Steven has that.

'He has been hugely experienced in his career in terms of being the leader in the dressing room, and I could tell quite quickly from some of the conversations we had in big moments that he was different to the normal person. Steven is extremely positive, really open, really wants to have a relationship with his players and is really open to ideas from his staff.'

As a player, Gerrard's mentality was without question. From the highs of Istanbul to the crushing lows of losing out on the Premier League title in 2014, he is famed for a never-say-die attitude that typifies British footballers throughout the last 20 to 30 years. There are many examples of great captains who go on to have less than stellar management careers, and it's a scenario where mentality, character and humility come to the fore.

Speaking to the *High Performance* podcast, Gerrard details a team meeting in the early weeks of his first pre-season at Rangers when he gave a speech on his vision:

'I remember addressing the squad after a few weeks. I wanted to let them know that I'm not addressing you as Steven Gerrard the player, this is me here to try and help and support you to try and improve you as a group. To use my experiences, my knowledge and my team as a group to be there for you and sacrifice everything individually and collectively to get you in a better place.

'We wanted to create a "no excuses" culture and the players had to buy into having their own accountability and responsibility.'

When asked how he approached the process of seeking buy-in from the players during those early weeks of pre-season in 2018, Gerrard said, 'Working with individuals takes time, it takes time to get to know them individually and time to build relationships and trust. One-on-one chats, getting to know people, show them what type of person I am away from football. Showing that I'm there for them and not in the role just for myself and my future as a manager. It's about the collective, what are we going to give to make this better and take this forward.'

From early on in Gerrard's first season, the manager identified players he felt should form the core of a dressing room 'leadership group' as he places great importance on a group that should be capable of running themselves. Being a captain at an elite club like Liverpool gave Gerrard a valuable insight into the other side of this relationship.

Throughout the early seasons at Rangers, the players' mentality was questioned intensely and regularly. Disappointing defeats in domestic cup competitions and the petering out of two title challenges following returns from the winter break had many people wondering whether this group had what it takes to do the hard yards and develop the consistency of mind required to take the next step.

Those criticisms were at their highest, and morale was arguably at its lowest, as Gerrard addressed the media following Rangers' defeat to Hearts at Tynecastle in early March 2020, which all but ended their hopes of any silverware for a second successive season.

'I need to think,' Gerrard said. 'The plan was to have a day off [on Sunday]. I need to think hard about where we are at as a group. I need to do some real, serious thinking in the next 24, 48 hours.'

Asked if that would include his own future, he replied, 'I just need to think. I need to think. I am feeling pain right now because I want to win here, and I am desperate to win here.

'Looking from the side today, I didn't get the impression that the feeling among my players was the same.

'I am not doubting myself. We have given these players everything, me and my staff have given these players absolutely everything for 20 months, held their hand on and off the pitch and improved everything for them.

'But it is tough when every other performance you feel the way you feel. It is tough. I need to analyse myself, for sure. This is the toughest moment I have had since I have come here.

'I think it will be extremely difficult in the short term [to win trophies] because of where we lie from a league point of view. We all know that we have punched above our weight in Europe so far, and this is what I need to analyse in the coming days.

'I'm very disappointed. It's the lowest I've felt since I came into the job by a long way.'

Rangers captain James Tavernier endured a tumultuous spell at the club since signing from Wigan for just £250,000 back in 2015.

Tavernier was the longest-serving player at the club throughout Gerrard's tenure, having been signed by Mark Warburton ahead of Rangers' second attempt to gain promotion from the Scottish Championship in 2015/16. No player sums up Rangers' journey more than Tavernier. Following Gerrard's arrival and receiving the captaincy, he went from strength to strength and had been the most important player at the club throughout. The journey to becoming a leader was something that Gerrard identified as possible within Tavernier even before he took over.

As the previous era limped to a close, Tavernier had been appointed as a temporary captain. Still, there were question marks over whether he was the right man to lead the Gerrard revolution. His new manager did not share those concerns.

'The gaffer says that the time that I've spent here and the work that I've done underneath him, he thought I was the right man to lead the boys,' said Tavernier.

'You always have to pinch yourself when you think about what the gaffer's thoughts are on who he'd give the captaincy to. It obviously was in the papers that he was going to think maybe of a new captain.

'I knew one of my ambitions was to captain the side one day. I've always seen myself as a leader and it's come at a perfect time.'

Connor Goldson was Tavernier's vice-captain, with the centre-back displaying what could be classed as more traditional leadership qualities as a defensive organiser. As would be expected, veteran goalkeeper Allan McGregor also formed part of the leadership group, with midfield trio Steven Davis, Scott Arfield and Ryan Jack. Together, this core of players had enormous amounts of elite-level experience and holistically understood the demands and expectations that came with being a Rangers player. They are the examples the team's younger members could not fail to look up to and be inspired by. The effect of this group symbolised the work done by the management team to instil the levels of mentality and character that would go on to make success possible.

Rangers showed immense character throughout this season. They not only won the title for the first time in ten years, but they did so by embarking on an unbeaten league campaign, only the fourth time this feat has ever been accomplished in Scottish domestic football. From 38 games played they drew just six and lost none, earning a club record total of 102 points. Indeed, in a show of complete dominance, Rangers found themselves in a losing position in league matches for a total of just 156 minutes over the course of the entire season.

A huge factor in this was the outstanding defensive displays, with the club breaking records left, right and centre. First, they broke the 117-year-old record of the number of clean sheets gained at the start of a Scottish league campaign, going seven games without conceding a goal. Next, Rangers broke the clean sheet record itself, becoming the first team to keep 26 clean sheets in a 38-game league campaign.

Lastly, they broke the British record for the number of goals conceded in a league campaign, letting in 13 with only one coming in 19 games at Ibrox. That British record of 15 goals against was set during José Mourinho's first season at Chelsea in 2004/05 and was deemed unlikely to be surpassed.

2

Formation Evolution

4-3-2-1 Origins

Football tactics and formations have been around for as long as football has. From 1-1-8 or 1-2-7 formations of the 1870s through to flexible, hybrid formations of the present day, interest and understanding of tactics has grown into an obsession for many football fans regardless of age or footballing knowledge. At the first sign of trouble in a game, we scream about changing formations and discuss whether teams should play three central midfielders to combat a superior opposition or go gung-ho and use an additional striker to take the game to them. We talk tactics without even really knowing we're doing it.

In the modern game, the adage that 'good players win you games' is no longer as accurate as it once was all those years ago. Players are still the decisive factor in most matches. The great managers of any era are those who are able to adapt to the ever-changing modern football landscape – they need to be constant revolutionaries in a world that doesn't always embrace change and innovation.

Still, throughout the decades, there are now countless examples of specific teams with a high level of tactical awareness achieving things that more talented groups of players playing in less effective tactical systems would not be capable of. Leicester City winning the Premier League in 2016 under Italian coach Claudio Ranieri showed that a robust tactical framework perfectly suited to a specific group of players can create something special.

Football is still primarily about finding ways to manipulate space to create a numerical advantage, but a solid tactical structure will allow you to achieve this in a multitude of different ways.

After a relatively barren spell, the 4-4-2 formation has been re-popularised in recent years through teams like Atlético Madrid and Leicester adopting it in very specific ways. Michael Cox's excellent book, *The Mixer*, looked at the history of Premier League tactics and described 4-4-2 as the de facto formation throughout the early 1990s and for several decades prior. On the continent, you were much more likely to see different tactical styles and approaches largely owing to the foreign influences and cultures that reached the major European leagues much quicker than they did the British game. The introduction of the back-pass rule in 1992 and some of those foreign visionaries such as Arsène Wenger arriving on these shores with more modern coaching techniques – and a more sophisticated viewpoint of the dietary requirements of footballers – started to shape the next generation of tactical evolution. In the English Premier League of today, we see the best coaches such as Pep Guardiola, Jürgen Klopp and Thomas Tuchel creating incredibly complex and layered tactical structures. These tactics are not only heavily tailored to suit the individual needs of specific teams and players but remain flexible enough to deal with almost every kind of opposition style they may face.

The 4-3-2-1 (Christmas Tree)

It has come to be known due to its shape when listed on the page but the Christmas tree formation has never been widely used as a default tactical shape. In many ways, this formation is just another iteration of 4-3-3, which again informs the opinion that the labels we give to where players stand on the pitch are not a useful guide to how a team play football. At its most basic form the 4-3-2-1 formation utilises a standard four-man defence with three central midfielders. This defensive base is one of the key benefits of the system, as the team become very difficult to attack centrally, thus forcing the opposition wide into less dangerous areas of the pitch. In turn, the only true width in an offensive sense comes from the full-backs, therefore the demands on the players in these roles is significant. The attacking three is primarily made up of two narrow supporting attackers behind a number nine or focal point, but each team will utilise this in different ways depending on the skillset or profile of players they have available to them, thus making this formation incredibly versatile if required.

Overall the Christmas tree formation can be classed as a very balanced tactical set-up with both the defensive and attacking areas of the team clearly segmented but also working well in tandem when required. The most obvious example of a team that lines up in a 4-3-2-1 formation would be Jürgen Klopp's Liverpool team, with rampaging full-back, supplying the team's width, a disciplined and functional midfield three and two inside-forwards working behind a central attacker. Sounds familiar, doesn't it? Throughout history there are several examples of the Christmas tree formation being used as a base, with tactical flexibility or uniqueness being introduced by way of seemingly minor tactical tweaks or the selection of a specific player.

Figure 9

France's 1998 World Cup-winning squad also adopted a 4-3-2-1 formation, but the philosophy behind this was less about the formation and more about the players at hand. Legendary French manager Aimé Jacquet had something that most managers aren't blessed with, the mercurial genius of then Juventus midfielder Zinedine Zidane. What Jacquet did was to devise a tactical plan that was built entirely around releasing Zizou from any defensive responsibilities as a way to ensure he was always best placed to affect the game in crucial areas of the pitch. Christian Karembeu, Emmanuel Petit and current

FRANCE

World Cup Final France 3-0 Brazil 12.07.98

The France 1998 4-3-2-1 was designed to retain defensive solidity whilst getting the most out of this team's star, Zinedine Zidane.

FIGURE 9

France manager Didier Deschamps provided the solid midfield three in this iteration with the primary function of protecting the defence. Still, while defensive solidity was the name of the game, these players were also given the freedom to roam forward as and when required. France only conceded two goals in their seven games en route to lifting the trophy, with Zidane enjoying the freedom of the Stade de France in the 3-0 demolition of Brazil in the final, finishing the game with two goals and a World Cup winners' medal.

A more recent French example of a variation on 4-3-2-1 could be found during their second World Cup win in 2018. In this instance, manager Deschamps selected then Juventus midfielder Blaise Matuidi in what could be classed as a nominally left-sided midfield role, but with the specific task of being a conduit between the team's defensive and attacking units.

'Matuidi brings much equilibrium to the team,' explained Deschamps. 'He is very effective, and plays with oomph. He covers a lot of ground, is an intense competitor and runs all day. He does his job at a very high level. He's an important part of our defensive solidity. All great teams have this and that's our strength.'

While Matuidi would be listed as a left-sided midfielder in this formation, he moved into more natural left central midfield roles throughout, creating a necessary balance throughout that dovetailed nicely with N'Golo Kanté and Paul Pogba while also allowing France's attackers the platform to do what they do best.

France won this World Cup by being defensively sound – again speaking to the defensive benefits of the Christmas tree formation – but only pressing when necessary and harnessing the fantastic ability and speed of Kylian Mbappé and Antoine Griezmann in the attack. Beale has referenced on several occasions how vital he believes the link between how you defend and how you attack should be and has cited this France team as an elite example of this.

Figure 10

The other prominent proponent of the Christmas tree formation is Carlo Ancelotti's AC Milan team of the early 2000s, who adopted this formation with great success both domestically and on the continent.

For a large part of his managerial career, Ancelotti was so convinced that the 4-3-2-1 was the best formation for an elite football team that he wrote a book, *Il Mio Albero Di Natale*, which took its title (*My Christmas Tree*) from the idea.

His first AC Milan team in the early 2000s would initially sacrifice all-natural width, a drastic move in an already narrow tactical set-up. In their 2003 Champions League-winning team, Ancelotti elected to play two converted centre-backs in Georgian Kakha Kaladze (now the mayor of Tbilisi) and legendary Italian defender Alessandro Costacurta as left- and right-full-backs respectively, making it clear how happy they were to concede possession on the flanks and rely on defensive play. Very classically Italian.

Of course, this was a few years before full-back play would be completely revolutionised, with these positions becoming de facto attackers in the modern game.

Figure 11

Again, the reasons for Ancelotti choosing the Christmas tree formation were not due to any ideological tendencies but instead the flexibility and control this shape allows. Ancelotti is famed for his ability to handle big players across a 30-year spell as manager at the cutting edge of European football. He can unfairly come across as a 'Mr Dependable' who will bow to star names and let them run roughshod over teams but the reality couldn't be further from the truth. Ancelotti's greatness and longevity at the top can be traced back to his tactical flexibility, aligned to his almost unparalleled man-management of those elite players. He is the master of taking over a team and devising a tactical approach to suit the players he currently has at his disposal.

FRANCE

World Cup Final France 4-2 Croatia 15.07.18

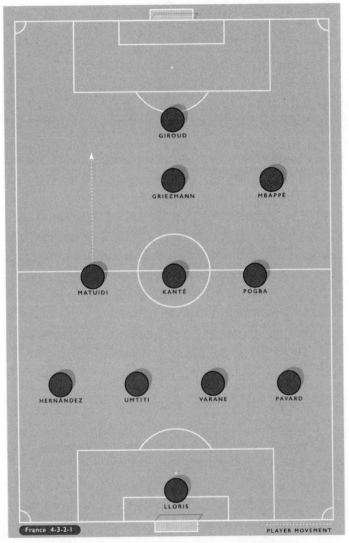

Blaise Matuidi acted as the conduit between France's solid midfield and their
star-studded front line.

FIGURE 10

AC MILAN

2003 Champions League Final AC Milan 0-0 Juventus (AC Milan win on penalties) 28.05.03

Carlo Ancelotti's first iteration of the Christmas tree sacrificed width in attack
in favour of more ball-playing midfielders.

FIGURE 11

Ancelotti's Milan iteration was borne from a desire to get as many ball players into his starting line-up as he possibly could. Andrea Pirlo, Clarence Seedorf and Rino Gattuso formed the central midfield, with Rui Costa and Kaká slotting in behind the lone striker, usually Andriy Shevchenko or Pippo Inzaghi.

This set-up allowed Ancelotti to make use of all his best players in the same team while still retaining the defensive strength that all great Italian teams are renowned for.

Figure 12

By the time of their 2007 triumph, AC Milan under Ancelotti were still setting up in a 4-3-2-1 formation with one clear difference. Their full-back play had evolved completely with legendary attacking right-back Cafu (backed up by Massimo Oddo) and two-footed Czech international Marek Jankulovski (a converted winger) providing their attacking width from the full-back areas. Selecting players with such a focused attacking profile in the full-back positions would become more and more popular as the years ticked past until it became as widely prevalent as to be the norm in the present day.

Ancelotti was willing to adapt and change in the wider defensive areas, but he remained obsessed with fitting in as many ball-playing central midfielders to the team as possible. He recognised the acute need for more defensive stability now he had such attacking full-backs and would frequently pair Massimo Ambrosini, Andrea Pirlo and Rino Gattuso in central midfield to provide more stability in a midfield three. Pirlo, at this stage, was not quite the classic regista he would go on to become, but nor was he a luxury attacking midfielder. These players were not required to provide much in the way of attacking thrust – box to box midfielders they were not – but they would provide the necessary protection for their centre-halves and shuttle out to cover their attacking full-backs should the situation demand it.

AC MILAN
2007 Champions League Final AC Milan 2-1 Liverpool 23.05.07

Four years later, Ancelotti again won the Champions League but this time
utilising attacking full-backs to provide the team's width.

FIGURE 12

Ahead of that midfield trio, Clarence Seedorf and Kaká formed the double number tens who were freed from defensive responsibility and encouraged to impact the game creatively as far up the pitch as possible in support of lone striker Pippo Inzaghi. Seedorf's flexibility and tactical awareness possibly summed up what Ancelotti looks for in a midfield player, with the Dutch international capable of playing in any of five positions in this formation and perhaps a couple more.

Figure 13

Of course, the most pertinent example of a team playing 4-3-2-1 would be the team that Steven Gerrard spent the majority of his playing career with. Liverpool under Jürgen Klopp have undertaken a remarkably similar tactical evolution to Gerrard's Rangers. The team that Klopp inherited just a few months following the end of Gerrard's playing career is unrecognisable from the squad that rampaged to Champions League and Premier League glory a few years later. Under Klopp's footballing philosophy, Liverpool's width and creativity comes primarily from two attacking full-backs who are relentless in dominating their respective flanks. In many ways, the skillsets of Trent Alexander-Arnold and Andy Robertson could be seen as similar to that of the Rangers incumbents, James Tavernier and Borna Barišić. Alexander-Arnold essentially plays the role of chief playmaker at Liverpool, notching high numbers of assists with his crossing ability while also retaining the ability to drive infield and create in the half-spaces. Andy Robertson plays a more traditional role on the opposite side similar to Barišić, with his technical ability on his left foot and crossing prowess the key standouts. In attack, they have a perfect blend of attacking talent with players such as Sadio Mané, Diogo Jota, Roberto Firmino and Mo Salah not only outstanding attackers in possession of the ball but also able to position themselves high and narrow on the pitch, ready to counter-press to usually devastating effect. This attacking power is ably supported by a

KLOPP'S LIVERPOOL
4-3-3

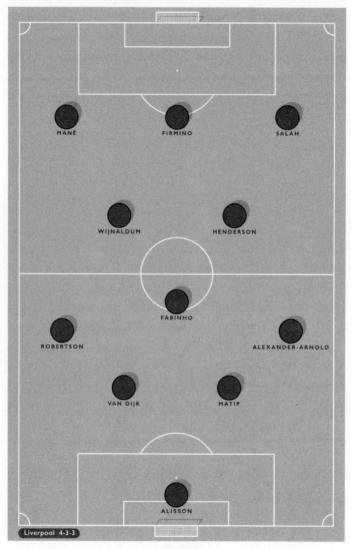

Jurgen Klopp's 4-3-3 has several tactical similarities with the 4-3-2-1 shape
Steven Gerrard adopted at Rangers.

FIGURE 13

functional midfield three with the primary focus on ensuring their shape remains narrow, balanced and compact in and out of possession, key tenets of the traditional 4-3-2-1 shape.

They had their challenges with breaking teams down in the early years of Klopp's time at Liverpool – similar to problems Gerrard faced at Rangers. But by continually tweaking and evolving his tactical set-up to ensure it was as flexible and balanced as it needed to be, Klopp would go on to huge success by winning the Premier League and the Champions League. It would be remiss to say otherwise, but signing high-quality players has a significant bearing on a team's performance and again this was the case here. In Brazilian goalkeeper Alisson and centre-back Virgil van Dijk, Liverpool paid big money for two players who would arguably go on to be the best in their position, in European football during this period. These players would fit seamlessly into the tactical set-up but also take the team on to the next level and, when added to the already scintillating array of attacking talent, they ensured that Liverpool were well primed to take those final successful steps.

In Liverpool, France and AC Milan, these are just some examples of successful teams who to the naked eye look to be playing very different playing styles, have very different players and indeed play these players in completely different roles. Still, to the casual observer, one thing was clear: they all lined up in a formation that didn't look too dissimilar to a Christmas tree.

Hibs 5 Rangers 5, 13 May 2018

Context is key in every discussion. Therefore, to fully understand the complete overhaul Steven Gerrard and his team oversaw throughout his first three years at Ibrox, there must be an understanding of where the club was at the point of his arrival in June 2018.

Jak Alnwick, James Tavernier, Andy Halliday, David Bates, Russell Martin, Jason Holt, Jordan Rossiter, Sean Goss, Daniel Candeias, Jason Murphy, Jason Cummings.

Figure 14

This was the final starting 11 selected in a competitive game prior to Gerrard taking charge. This match came just nine days after his unveiling at a press conference at Ibrox, where he spoke in depth about his desire to succeed at Rangers and his ambition to relaunch the club. Rangers' next outing and Gerrard's first match in charge – a 2-0 win against FC Shkupi in the Europa League first qualifying round – would come just 60 days later, on 12 July. A short number of days may have elapsed, but the turnaround in personnel on the bench and in the starting XI was apparent straight from the off. Indeed, in that game against Shkupi, Tavernier, Murphy, and Candeias were the only survivors in the starting 11 from the previous match against Hibs, which shows the scale of the overhaul even at this embryonic stage.

The 2017/18 season was a wretched one for Rangers which saw them humiliated in the first round of Europa League

HIBERNIAN 5-5 RANGERS

SPFL Easter Road 13.05.18

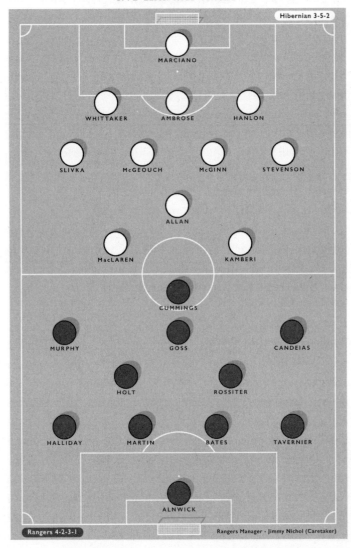

The final line-up of the pre-Gerrard era as season 2017/18 limped to a close.

FIGURE 14

qualifying, losing 2-1 on aggregate to Progrès Niederkorn. Domestically, an awful campaign littered with poor performance, and managerial changes saw them finish third in the league for the second season running following their promotion back to the top flight in 2016. Those first two years back in the Scottish Premiership had been punishing in more ways than one, as there had been a perhaps unfair pressure – especially when you consider the vast gap in finances available to both clubs – on the team to immediately challenge for the title and halt Celtic's supposed procession towards ten in a row. As Rangers limped to the end of the season – three points behind Aberdeen and 12 behind seven-in-a-row champions Celtic – it was difficult to see any ray of light.

The defeats to Celtic were crushing and demoralising but ultimately not hugely surprising given the financial disparity between the two teams. In the season previous, Celtic were revitalised after a few years without a challenge in the top flight. They had just finished an unbeaten season under Brendan Rodgers, with draws in only four games, giving them a record points tally of 106. A title challenge may have seemed fanciful to most in hindsight, but there was absolutely no excuse for Rangers not to be comfortably finishing second in what still should have been a two-horse race. On 1 May 2018, Graeme Murty was relieved of his duties following two defeats against Celtic by an aggregate score of 9-0. Then the assistant manager and former Rangers defender, Jimmy Nichol, picked up the reins for the remaining three games of the season. Nichol was Rangers' third manager of that season following the sacking of Pedro Caixinha and the long, fruitless hunt for a replacement before Murty was re-appointed as caretaker.

Nichol's final match in charge was an incredible 5-5 draw with Hibernian at Easter Road. The game acted as a perfect microcosm of the previous three years and, therefore, it was quite fitting that it ended more than one era. Rangers were three down to Hibs after just 22 minutes with all the goals coming due to some less-than-stellar defending. A soft centre of defence was something that had plagued Rangers throughout these early seasons back in the top flight and it would be something that Gerrard would immediately rectify in the transfer market. Despite a remarkable comeback – Josh Windass scored to give Rangers a 5-3 lead in the 68th minute – these defensive frailties came to the fore twice more later in the game, giving the match its final result.

Under the stewardship of Murty, in his second spell as caretaker manager in as many years, Rangers were a team who could be good on their day but lacked the quality on the pitch to impose themselves on the league. This meant Murty could not turn the team into a consistent force capable of putting together the volume of victories required to become champions. However, there was a period where the team did threaten Celtic briefly, hope that was extinguished by an agonising 3-2 defeat to Celtic at Ibrox in March 2018. A victory in this game would have given Rangers their eighth win in ten league games and taken them to within three points of their rivals with eight matches left, albeit Celtic still had one more to play.

Despite leading twice and Celtic losing Croatian centre-back Jozo Šimunović to a red card before the hour mark, Rangers fell short, and their unlikely title charge was over. Liverpool youth coach Steven Gerrard was also present at this game, with his young side in Glasgow to play their Rangers peers, and just six weeks later he would be announced as the Ibrox club's new manager.

Former Scotland international defender Murty retired as a player in 2010 and held youth developmental roles at the academies of Southampton and Norwich before being appointed head coach for the development squad at Rangers in August 2016. Upon his promotion to first-team coach, Murty's Rangers elected to play in a standard 4-2-3-1 shape predicated on getting balls wide and attacking at pace on the counter. The inability to properly influence the centre of the pitch would be symptomatic of Murty's tactical approach and is at odds with the generally accepted principle that controlling this area is key to success. Rangers undoubtedly had talented attacking options at full-back and in the final third, and for a period, Murty's tactics appeared to make the most of these strengths.

Figure 15

This is the side that took to the field against Aberdeen in January 2018. Tavernier and Candeias's fledgling relationship down the right was a key strength of Rangers' attack this season and would go on to be so again into the next era under Gerrard. On the other side, Declan John was not without fault but provided a decent option on the ball and worked well with Jamie Murphy as the left-sided attacker.

Josh Windass finished the season with 19 goals and five assists in competitive games. Playing in arguably his best position as a number ten, he could be satisfied with his return despite the overall team performance. Similarly, in his debut campaign at Ibrox, Alfredo Morelos racked up 16 goals and five assists of his own. Overall, Rangers scored 76 league goals, the most in the division and three more than champions Celtic. Scoring goals and creating chances was certainly not the issue despite the continual flux of this season.

Ultimately, Rangers' lack of proven quality in vital central areas would prove to be their undoing. After his summer arrival from Aberdeen, Ryan Jack's debut season ended on 27 December 2017 following an injury during a 2-0 win against Motherwell at Ibrox. By way of context, throughout the rest of Murty's time in charge of the first team, his central midfield options consisted of Graham Dorrans, Jason Holt, Andy Halliday, Sean Goss and Greg Docherty. At centre-back, Rangers mainly utilised David Bates, Ross McCrorie, Danny Wilson and the ageing duo of Bruno Alves and Russell Martin.

Rangers' defensive frailties were not contained solely to the centre of the pitch, with the team frequently conceding high-

RANGERS 2-0 ABERDEEN
SPFL Ibrox Stadium 24.01.18

A typical Rangers line up in season 2017/18 under Graeme Murty.

FIGURE 15

quality chances and goals from crosses into the box, primarily from the left flank. Due to the nature of a tactical set-up that was so focused on counter-attacking at pace with little in the way of defensive structure, gaps will always begin to appear. As outlined in earlier chapters, teams who can win the ball back through counter-pressing and attack are far more likely to gain an attacking advantage in these situations. In 2017/18, Rangers conceded on average ten shots per game with approximately 40 per cent of these on target, with a significant number of goals conceded due to counter-attacks.

Rangers conceded 50 goals in their 38 league games in 2017/18, more than any of the other top seven teams that season. This was the most conceded in the league by a Rangers team in the top flight since they let in 51 in 1958/59 under Scot Symon. On the most basic levels, it was clear which area of the team the incoming manager would look to address first.

In new club captain Tavernier, midfield lynchpin Ryan Jack, Candeias and Colombian striker Alfredo Morelos, Rangers had players who would go on to be successful with the club but required a much more structured tactical approach to excel in and, more importantly, a severe upgrade in the quality of their on-pitch support.

Rangers' first four signings of the Gerrard era were defensive players; therefore, it is clear that while Gerrard and his team may have only been at the club for a matter of weeks, they had quickly identified strengthening the defence as a key pillar of the rebuild. The early recruitment swiftly addressed these glaring deficiencies within the team.

2018 Squad Overview

Under Gerrard, it's widely acknowledged that Rangers played a variation of a standard 4-3-3 formation. The formation has developed throughout but it has been a case of evolution rather than revolution, with the base shape in and out of possession remaining similar throughout.

In this section of the book, I will attempt to bring to life the tactical theory introduced in part one to chart the year-on-year evolution of the Rangers starting 11 by providing a high-level overview of two key themes outlined throughout. Firstly, by reviewing what the addition of new players can bring to their team and then by analysing the impact their specific skillsets had on the team each season. Throughout this section, I will introduce some of the tactical evolutions that will be explored in more detail later in the book.

With that aforementioned focus on the need for defensive improvements, Rangers goalkeeping legend Allan McGregor returned on a free transfer from Hull City. McGregor had left the club during the travails of 2012 and following a short spell in Turkey with Beşiktaş, he settled on the banks of the river Humber and into Premier League life. Following Hull's relegation in season 2017/18, the then 36-year-old jumped at the chance to rejoin his boyhood club and became the first signing of the Gerrard era. In McGregor, Rangers had recruited an excellent goalkeeper who not only represented a significant upgrade on the existing number one, Wes Foderingham, but crucially he also understood the pressure and demands of the club and had the necessary experience of winning leagues during his trophy-laden first spell.

Brighton & Hove Albion defender Connor Goldson, 25, also signed for approximately £3.5m. Goldson, a ball-playing centre-back who had come through the ranks at Shrewsbury Town, playing for a short spell with his future captain Tavernier, joined from Premier League side Brighton in search of regular first-team football. The boyhood Liverpool fan was enticed north to Glasgow with the aid of a personal visit to his home by the new manager. Goldson was keen to get back playing football regularly after almost two full seasons out following the discovery of a heart defect and subsequent preventative surgery. Following his recovery, the centre-half had been on the fringes of the Brighton team and the opportunity at Ibrox was one he felt he could not turn down.

Goldson was joined by 21-year-old Croatian Niko Katić as the pair formed the new centre-back partnership. Despite having one cap to his name – won in a late substitute appearance in a friendly against Mexico the previous year – this signing seemed to come from nowhere and on the face of it appeared to be an example of Rangers' scouting network starting to grow to a level that would be expected for a club of this size. Katić was signed from Slaven Belupo in his homeland and would quickly endear himself to fans with his never-say-die attitude to defending. Despite his young age, Katić had been a regular for Slaven in the Croatian Prva HNL for two seasons before his transfer to Rangers.

Another Croatian was added to the team once the season had begun in the shape of 25-year-old left-back Borna Barišić, the second of three summer signings from Croatia, joining from NK Osijek. This deal was a little more akin to what Rangers fans were used to as throughout the club's modern history, it appeared that any opposition player who had a good game against Rangers would inevitably be linked with a transfer to the club. Just five days prior to his £1.5m move, Rangers had defeated Barišić's team in the Europa League second qualifying round at Ibrox with Barišić putting in a fantastic performance as an attack-minded left-back, culminating in scoring a late consolation goal at Ibrox for the visitors to draw the second leg 1-1. Barišić even went as far as spending a portion of this match wearing a bandage on his head following a collision that required treatment. Rangers, of course, have a long affinity with players who wear head bandages from another Croatian, striker Dado Pršo, back to England veteran Terry Butcher in the late 1980s. While this may have been a coincidence, it was still a nice link to previous eras.

Jon Flanagan, a versatile 25-year-old full-back, joined on a free transfer from Liverpool. Flanagan was a former team-mate of Gerrard at Anfield and a player the manager knew very well. In a summer of much upheaval, having someone who could play on both flanks would be highly advantageous, with Flanagan starting the campaign as the first-choice left-back and going on to make 30 appearances in all competitions throughout his debut season.

In central midfield, Canadian international Scott Arfield was the first player to join the Gerrard revolution as the 29-year-old signed on 14 May 2018 on a free transfer from Premier League side Burnley. Arfield would go on to make the most significant impact in this season, playing as a box-to-box midfielder capable of getting into the penalty area by utilising clever runs and combination play, particularly with Morelos. Prior to signing for Rangers, Arfield had spent five years at Burnley playing in both the Championship and the Premier League. Usually deployed in a narrow left-sided midfield role with a more defensive focus due to Burnley's tactical set-up, Arfield adapted well to receiving more of the ball at Rangers and the attacking demands placed on him.

Rangers bolstered their ranks further with the permanent signings of ex-West Bromwich Albion centre-back Gareth McAuley, Bosnian winger Eros Grezda and ex-Ranger Kyle

Lafferty. The club also confirmed Jamie Murphy's permanent deal from Brighton following his loan to buy agreement in the previous January.

Gerrard, sporting director Mark Allen and chief scout Andy Scoulding also delved into their contacts book, to bring in young Liverpool duo Ovie Ejaria and Ryan Kent on loan. Both players arrived with significant expectation given the deep connections that the coaching staff had with their parent club. Further temporary deals for Nottingham Forest centre-back Joe Worrall, Mali international midfielder Lassana Coulibaly from Angers and the young Roma forward Umar Sadiq were also confirmed as the squad started to take shape throughout the rest of the summer transfer window.

Of the five loanees signed in this window, Kent and Ejaria would make the biggest impact in this first season, with both players trusted from the off having spent time working under Michael Beale during their time at the Anfield academy. Ejaria was a languid central midfielder with excellent close control and awareness of space around him and will be remembered most fondly for his goal against Russian team Ufa in the Europa League play-off round second leg, which sent Rangers through to the group stages. Incredibly, they achieved this feat with nine men for the last half an hour of the second leg, having lost Alfredo Morelos to a first-half red card and Jon Flanagan joining him shortly after half-time. In qualifying – courtesy of Ejaria's excellent goal – Rangers became one of just four teams to reach the group stages having started their campaigns in the first qualifying round that season. The importance of this from a sporting viewpoint is obvious, but the financial benefit also should not be understated as this provided the club with much needed funds at a crucial time in their rebuild.

In Kent, Rangers had a precocious 21-year-old left-winger who had bounced around several loan clubs in the previous seasons, with a Young Player of the Year award at Barnsley in 2016/17 being the major highlight. He played predominantly on the left for Rangers during his initial season; Kent's pace and two-footed ability were a real highlight of the attacking play, especially when supplemented by his tenacity, desire out of possession and willingness to do the hard yards for the good of the team. A terrific assist for Ryan Jack's goal in a December victory over Celtic and a fantastic all-round performance further endeared him to the fanbase in a way that only performances in Old Firm games can.

In total, during that frantic first transfer window, the club made 15 first team signings for a combined transfer outlay of approximately £11m. Ten players left permanently, with Josh Windass (£2.5m to Wigan) and Declan John (£500,000 to Swansea) the only ones sold for a transfer fee. An additional seven faces who had featured under the previous regime including Carlos Peña, Jason Holt and Eduardo Herrera would leave the club on loan as the first building blocks of the Gerrard revolution started to take shape.

Figure 16

Following that 1-0 victory against Celtic on Saturday, 29 December 2018 – the first win against their Old Firm rivals in 13 games – Rangers found themselves level on points at the top of the league despite having played one game more as they entered the winter shutdown.

Rangers strengthened further in the January transfer window with the vastly experienced duo of Northern Ireland central midfielder Steven Davis – the third ex-Ranger to rejoin the club this season – and hugely experienced England striker Jermain Defoe joining on loan from Southampton and Bournemouth respectively. The signing of Kyle Lafferty had not produced performances to the required standard, therefore the signing of Defoe was a necessary one to reduce the goalscoring burden on Alfredo Morelos.

Like Allan McGregor, Davis had enjoyed enormous success with Rangers in his first spell, winning eight major honours and

RANGERS 5 - 1 ST JOHNSTONE
SPFL Ibrox Stadium 23.09.18

The huge turnaround in playing staff under Steven Gerrard was evident just a few weeks into the domestic season.

FIGURE 16

playing a key role in the club's incredible run to the UEFA Cup Final in 2008. Davis rejoined having just turned 34 and, having barely featured in the 12 months prior, there were question marks over whether he could provide what Rangers needed in midfield. As with most central midfield players, Davis's role had evolved as he got older at Southampton. When he left Rangers, Davis was an energetic, box-to-box-style individual also capable of playing on the right of midfield should the situation demand it, but the player who rejoined the club was a much more mature and defensive-minded playmaker.

Dundee central midfielder and Finnish international Glen Kamara signed a pre-contract agreement in January, with the move made permanent later in the window for the princely sum of £50,000. This signing was noted at the time as being very prudent by the club, with the ex-Arsenal man clearly a level above most non-Old Firm players in the Scottish league. Kamara, 23, had been a graduate of the Arsenal academy before leaving in 2017 in search of first-team football following loan spells at Southend and Colchester United. Ex-Rangers winger Neil McCann was in charge of SPFL side Dundee at the time and brought Kamara north on a two-year deal where he came to the attention of the Ibrox club, impressing throughout his 18 months on Tayside. Describing Kamara's style is a complex task. Not quite a defensive midfielder, nor an attacking midfielder and not particularly adept as a playmaker, Kamara just knits things together in a way that can be undervalued. There are genuinely very few players in the game who have a similar profile to his. As we will delve into in later chapters, he possesses a wide range of skills which mean he has the flexibility to impress in many different in-game scenarios.

Loan duo Ejaria and Sadiq returned to their parent clubs as both ultimately failed to settle during their time at Rangers.

The illustration overleaf details how Rangers' tactical shape evolved under Gerrard in those early months. This shows the average pass locations from the 0-0 draw away to Hibernian in December 2018, when Rangers dominated but ultimately could not find a cutting edge in front of goal.

Figure 17

Full-backs and wingers were tasked with staying wide to stretch play and provide the bulk of the creativity. Their role was primarily to get down the wing as quickly as possible and deliver balls into the box. With Borna Barišić and James Tavernier supporting Daniel Candeias and Ryan Kent or ex-Norwich youngster Glenn Middleton, it was clear from the early months that crossing was a prominent feature of Rangers' play under Gerrard. Pressing and aggression were a much more prominent feature of the team's play this season, with the tactical set-up arguably more of a counter-attacking style at times with the stated aim of hassling and harrying teams into giving up the ball in dangerous areas where Rangers could then utilise their pace on the break to dangerous effect.

Rangers finished the first half of the season level on points with arch-rivals Celtic courtesy of the aforementioned Ryan Jack goal in a 1-0 win at Ibrox on 29 December 2018. Following this game and heading into the winter break, it was felt that Rangers had 'set down a marker' against Celtic and hoped to return refreshed and ready to mount a serious title challenge. In the Europa League group stage, Rangers had perhaps shown their understandable inexperience at this level, finishing in third place exiting Europe, behind Villarreal and Rapid Vienna but ahead of Spartak Moscow. Creditable draws home and away with Villarreal and a fantastic 3-1 victory against Rapid Vienna at home were an insight into things to come in future Europa League campaigns.

As Rangers evolved throughout the three years, their style of play developed into a more controlled approach with more possession, and a natural decline in the intensity of their pressing was noticeably evident. As a team becomes more successful, this

HIBERNIAN 0 - 0 RANGERS
SPFL Easter Road 19.12.18

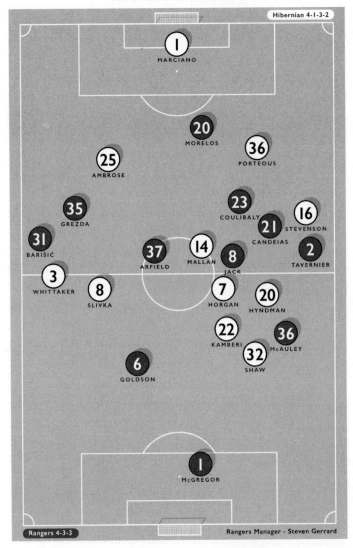

The average pass locations from Ranger's draw with Hibernian showed a clear 4-3-3 identity.

FIGURE 17

is a natural tendency as opponents will look to sit deeper and attempt to frustrate the more dominant team.

These changes manifested themselves on the pitch in two major ways. Firstly, through a series of seemingly minor tactical tweaks and secondly, the introduction of new players who would align more closely with the style the coaching team were trying to implement. The midfield three evolved throughout this season but the biggest shift was the switch from a traditional defensive midfield destroyer to a deeper-lying playmaker. This change came through the replacement of Ross McCrorie – who provided a solid if not outstanding base and performed a vital role in breaking up play and feeding the ball to the wide players – with Steven Davis following his return to Ibrox. The further addition of Kamara in January in place of the now-departed Ovie Ejaria again added a different skillset to that left-sided central midfield role. When Davis and Kamara combined with Ryan Jack as the first-choice midfield, this allowed Rangers to play three ball-players in the middle of the park, thus ensuring their ability to keep possession was maximised. However, one continued criticism of this midfield three throughout this season was that they were nowhere near as involved in the attacking third of the pitch as you would expect a central midfield to be. Despite this tweak to add more finesse to the middle of the pitch, throughout the vast majority of Gerrard's first season at the club, Rangers would continue to remain focused mainly on attacking down the flanks, utilising the skills of both sets of full-backs and wingers.

The attacking set-up was primarily focused on providing ammunition to the number nine, Alfredo Morelos, who continued to be a constant thorn in all opposition defenders' sides (sometimes taking on entire defences single-handedly). Morelos favoured dropping into the right half-space to rotate and combine effectively with Tavernier and Candeias; however, he tended to become isolated and was forced to try and feed off scraps. Along with the goalkeeper, this role is possibly the only one within the team that did not evolve hugely following the summer of 2018. Still, Morelos has developed significantly as a player and continues to grow into his position.

Despite starting 2019 level on points with Celtic and adding Kamara, Davis and Defoe to the team, Rangers endured a poor run of league results with just five wins in their first ten fixtures, ending in a narrow 2-1 loss to Celtic in March 2019 that put paid to any fledgling title hopes they may have had. Alfredo Morelos was sent off in this game, and this meant that the management team were faced with a problem, which they duly turned into an opportunity. Jermain Defoe was the obvious striker replacement but his skillset – other than his goalscoring capability – was entirely different to that of Morelos. Defoe has always been a supreme goalscorer and this was still the case even at the ripe old age of 36 but one thing he had never been, was a player who was hugely involved in dropping deep and contributing to his team's build-up play in the way that Alfredo Morelos could. Conversely, Defoe – standing at just 5ft 7in tall – isn't a player you would look towards in order to make something happen from endless crosses into the box.

With that in mind, Rangers switched to a 4-3-2-1 formation for the remainder of the league season, with the two wingers being asked to play narrower as a means to provide additional support to Defoe as the lone striker. This tweak gave Rangers significantly increased flexibility in the final third and allowed them to attack the opposition from central areas by finding pockets of space between the lines.

The tactical adjustment yielded significant success with a six-game winning run – their best of the season – towards the end of the campaign. Despite the season ending trophyless again – Rangers would lose to Aberdeen in the League Cup semi-final and again at Ibrox in the Scottish Cup quarter-final – there was sufficient optimism and intrigue surrounding this new tactical approach and the possibilities that summer additions to the playing squad could take Rangers to the next level.

Figure 18

RANGERS' 'TWIN TENS'

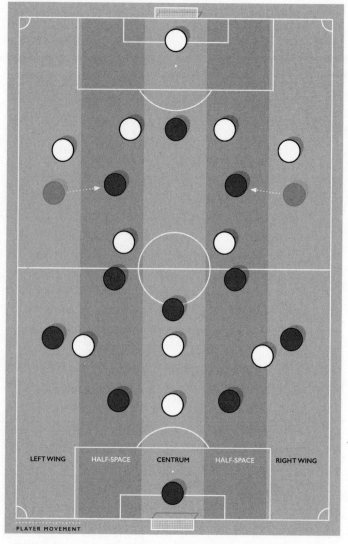

In a bid to gain more control and provide better support to Morelos in the final third, Rangers switched from a traditional 4-3-3 to a 4-3-2-1 by asking their wingers to play narrower as 'twin tens'.

FIGURE 18

2019 Squad Overview

Figure 19

In Gerrard's second season in charge, Rangers' attacking shape and cohesion was significantly enhanced by several intrinsically related factors. The evolutions in midfield and within the front three introduced in the closing weeks of the previous season were now embedded and starting to bear fruit tactically. Still, as always, players play the most significant role in any team's success. The return of Morelos following his lengthy suspension at the end of the previous season proved a key factor as he took to this new tactical shape with significant ease. The shape change benefited the Colombian greatly as he was less reliant on service from deep and instead had central runners who would benefit from his ability to attract defenders to him, thus creating space in their defensive structure to be exploited. As the transfer window neared its close in late August 2019, Morelos had already scored ten goals and provided three assists in his first 11 games, including a last-gasp winner in the second leg of Rangers' Europa League play-off round. This match against Legia Warsaw was pivotal in late August as it again sealed progression to the group stages for the second season in a row and unlocked the aforementioned additional financial benefits.

Therefore, European qualification once again allowed Rangers to invest heavily and this was born out in the next few days. In the final hours of the transfer window, Rangers clinched the permanent transfer of Ryan Kent from Liverpool for £7.5m – a huge transfer fee for the club at any time in their

RANGERS 5-0 HEARTS

SPFL Ibrox Stadium 01.12.19

Rangers' signings in both 2019 transfer windows had a sizeable impact
on the quality and tactical approach of the team.

FIGURE 19

history never mind at this stage. However, the player in question was less of a gamble, as Rangers knew exactly the potentially transformative performances they could expect from Kent from his time on loan in the previous season. Following an injury-hit second debut, it would be late October before Kent rejoined the team regularly and he would waste no time in picking up where he left off in what was now a left-sided number ten role on the pitch.

The other big-money signing of the summer came in mid-July in the shape of 26-year-old Swedish international Filip Helander, who joined from Serie A club Bologna for £3.5m. Helander – a left-footed centre-back of significant top-level experience – provided a balance to the defence and more importantly some serious competition for Niko Katić that was sorely lacking, particularly with Gareth McAuley and loanee Joe Worrall leaving at the end of the previous season.

Despite his obvious pedigree, coming through at Malmö before spending four seasons first with Verona and latterly Bologna, Helander would have to be patient to force his way into the team. Indeed, regular game time was not forthcoming until the opening game of that season's Europa League group campaign, the 1-0 win against Feyenoord on 19 September 2019. Until the Swede's season-ending injury in the 1-0 League Cup Final loss to Celtic in early December – a match that Rangers dominated thoroughly, missing a hatful of chances including a penalty – Helander and Goldson formed a formidable partnership as Rangers enjoyed their best run of form in the 18 months since Gerrard joined.

George Edmundson joined for a fee of approximately £600,000 from Oldham and would again add to the options in central defence. The 21-year-old would make 15 appearances throughout his time at the club and looked to have some promise as a centre-back, arguably ending the COVID-disrupted season as first choice partner to Goldson, thus moving Katić even further down the pecking order. Edmundson would also score the consolation goal in Rangers' final game of that season, a 3-1 defeat to Bayer Leverkusen in the last 16 of the Europa League.

The final transfer fee paid this summer was for 23-year-old Nigerian midfield Joe Aribo, with Rangers taking advantage of the cross-border 'loophole' to sign the player upon the expiration of his contract with Charlton Athletic, who had just been promoted to the English Championship. Then Charlton manager Lee Bowyer was scathing in his assessment of Aribo's decision, primarily due to the perceived quality of the Scottish league. In his first two seasons at the club, Aribo became a mainstay of the team, performing to a high level in the latter stages of the Europa League and ultimately winning a league title. Allied to that, Aribo became a full international with Nigeria and evolved into a key player for the Super Eagles over that two-year period.

The introduction of Aribo – and Ianis Hagi in the January transfer window – gave Rangers a new dimension as both players were capable of playing in a variety of positions due to the hybrid nature of their technical skillsets. The first Old Firm game of 2019/20 saw Aribo and Arfield lining up as the number tens behind Jermain Defoe. Despite losing this match, it was clear to see that Gerrard and Beale were looking for ways to evolve Rangers' final-third play and firmly move away from the traditional wingers. As Borna Barišić started to make the left-back slot his own, it would be the Croatian and Tavernier on the right-hand flank who would become the team's primary source of width.

The remaining signings in the summer transfer window were a combination of loans and free transfers, with Rangers looking to improve the depth of talent available to the manager. Steven Davis joined following his relatively successful six-month loan spell, signing an initial one-year contract following the expiration of his Southampton deal. The club also loaned in Premier League-winning Leicester City midfielder Andy King to reinforce the midfield options following the departures of

Lassana Coulibaly, Ovie Ejaria and Ross McCrorie. Excitement around this signing was palpable, given King's exploits just a few seasons earlier with Leicester, but unfortunately the Welshman would fail to make an impact, making just five appearances in total during his six-month stay.

Rangers again utilised the Liverpool connection to bring in England under-21 international winger Sheyi Ojo in this window. Ojo made a promising start to his time at Ibrox, becoming a regular in the side throughout the season's early stages and chipping in with some valuable goal contributions, none more so than an emphatic finish to give Rangers a 1-0 victory against Feyenoord in that Europa League group stage encounter. His tendency to shoot when the opportunity presented itself was a breath of fresh air at times in the early weeks of 2019/20, particularly in this new narrow front three that had not always been as prolific as they could be. The team had been hugely reliant on Alfredo Morelos to score goals in both of the last two seasons, so another player who could potentially share the attacking burden was highly sought after. In his first 20 appearances, Ojo racked up five goals and five assists, with the last of these coming in a 4-0 victory away to Ross County in October 2019. As the weeks and months progressed his decision-making became more erratic and unfortunately, his remaining 15 matches yielded no further goal contributions as his impact on games and minutes in the team gradually reduced due to the re-emergence of Ryan Kent.

Jordan Jones, Greg Stewart, Jake Hastie and Brandon Barker all joined on free transfers as players who it could reasonably be assumed, would offer competition for the number ten roles. The first three players were signed from within the domestic league and had at times played well against Rangers over the club's recent history. In that sense, these signings at relatively low cost possibly made sense but as we would find out, there is a sizeable difference between playing well against Rangers and the expectation of playing for Rangers. Of that quartet, only Stewart had any experience of playing as a number ten; therefore, it could be argued that the team retained the flexibility to revert to the formation of the previous year if the situation demanded it. Similarly, it could be argued that the club's recruitment of these players was more than a little strange, as they had now signed three wingers for a new system which did not use that type of player.

Jones was arguably the most anticipated of these four signings, with the ex-Kilmarnock winger proving to be a thorn in Rangers' side on more than one occasion during his time with the Ayrshire club. Questions remained as to whether Jones's style of play aligned to Rangers, with the Northern Irishman more comfortable playing on the counter-attack to utilise his searing pace. Jones started his time in a promising manner as he played a key role in the 4-2 victory away to FC Midtjylland and provided the cross for Morelos's late winner against Legia Warsaw at Ibrox. Unfortunately, he injured himself making a late, ill-timed tackle on Celtic full-back Moritz Bauer in the very next game, a 2-0 loss at Ibrox. The red card and subsequent injury lay-off put paid to his hopes of making any consistent impact on the team throughout that season.

The club continued to try to offload players deemed surplus to requirements with Lee Hodson, Kyle Lafferty, Jak Alnwick, Jordan Rossiter, Lee Wallace, Jason Holt, Eduardo Herrera, Joe Dodoo, Graham Dorrans and Gareth McAuley all leaving either on loans or free transfers. A surprise departure was Daniel Candeias, with the Portuguese winger playing a pivotal role in Gerrard's first season. With an incredible seven of the players signed in this window capable of playing in attacking positions behind the central striker, 31-year-old Candeias joined the Turkish Super Lig team Gençlerbirliği for around £250,000. He was a loss, but the player himself admitted he needed to be guaranteed first-team football at that stage of his career.

Rangers started the 2019/20 season like a train, only dropping seven points from their first 19 games. Again the final game prior to the break would be against Celtic, and again Rangers would be victorious, this time winning 2-1 at Parkhead with goals from Niko Katić and Ryan Kent sealing the win in a fiery encounter.

In Europe, Rangers enjoyed huge success by finishing second in a very difficult Europa League group featuring Porto, Feyenoord and Young Boys. Rangers beat Porto and Feyenoord in pulsating matches at Ibrox before securing creditable away draws against the pair to seal post-Christmas European football against all the odds. A key factor in this successful campaign was the solid defensive base that the midfield trio of Steven Davis, Ryan Jack and Glen Kamara imbued on the team. This tactical tweak aligned nicely to Michael Beale's focus on keeping a 'narrow and compact defensive shape'.

Their roles cannot be underestimated as they essentially created a solid line of three in midfield rather than a traditional defensive midfielder behind two box-to-box players. This allowed them to cover the full-backs' forward runs by shuffling over laterally while maintaining a solid defensive structure in front of the centre-backs.

Figure 20

In the January 2020 window, Rangers again added two players capable of playing in the attacking roles, with young Romanian number ten Ianis Hagi joining on an initial loan with the option to buy from Belgian team KRC Genk. Not only was his father Gheorghe the most famous Romanian player of all time, but 21-year-old Hagi junior had impressed at the UEFA European Under-21 Championship the previous summer as Romania reached the semi-finals. Also joining was Swiss striker Florian Kamberi, who signed late in the window on a six-month loan from Hibernian as Rangers again tried to search valiantly for a player who could share the goalscoring burden with Morelos.

Hagi would immediately positively impact the team, playing as a right-sided number ten and scoring a wonderfully taken

FLAT MIDFIELD THREE

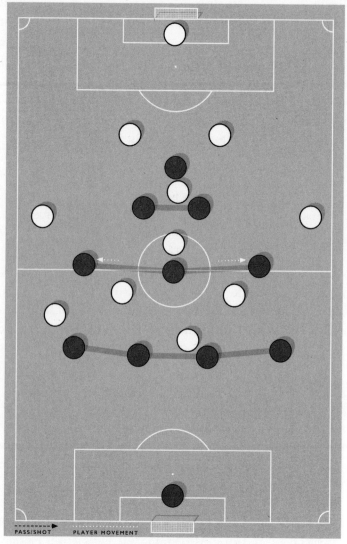

The wide central midfielders played a vital role out of possession, forming as a solid central defensive base but often moving wide to provide support to the attacking full-backs.

FIGURE 20

goal on his full debut as he showcased his two-footed ability to seal three late points against Hibernian at Ibrox. Hagi would show his class again in the last 32 of the Europa League against Portuguese team Braga, memorably scoring two goals in a home leg which Rangers ended up winning 3-2 despite trailing 2-0 with just 23 minutes remaining. Rangers would go on to win the away leg too, with Hagi's vision coming to the fore as he set up Kent to score the only goal of the game and secure progress to the last 16. As mentioned on page 103, Rangers lost the home leg 3-1 to Leverkusen in the final match prior to the season being curtailed.

Both Hagi and Kamberi joined at a difficult time for the club as again Rangers returned from the winter break and straight into some awful domestic form. That 2-1 win at Parkhead was the first at that venue in ten years, but Rangers again restarted their league campaign following the winter shutdown poorly in what was fast becoming an unwanted tradition. Following that victory, Rangers were two points behind Celtic with a game in hand and appeared to have the initiative in the title race. Rangers would win just five of their ten games following, collecting 17 points from a possible 30 to hand the advantage back to their city rivals.

The progression in the first season under Gerrard had been undeniable, but at a club like Rangers, standing still is never a viable option. Throughout the manager's second season in charge, several tactical improvements were introduced to ensure Rangers continued to progress forward on the right path.

'It's important to have players who can outplay their opponent one on one and provoke the block to take on the first player. We work a lot on combination play, trying to cross early to put defenders under pressure. It comes down to a matter of taking chances and having moments of quality. There have been key games this season where we've encountered low blocks and done fantastically well taking chances,' said first team coach Michael Beale in a 2019 interview with Rangers TV.

The flexibility of Gerrard's tactical philosophy again came to the fore, with the management team adhering to those fundamental principles while simultaneously implementing tweaks as and when required to suit the myriad of challenges the team may face.

The addition of so many options in the attacking roles resulted in Rangers performing very well when faced with teams who sat deep and frustrated, something that the tactical set-up of the previous year had clearly struggled with. It's undeniable that a Rangers team playing in Scotland will come up against many, many more games against opponents who will pack defences in this way, so figuring out how to get the better of these teams and beat the low block was crucial going into this season.

Figure 21

The image next page across shows the average pass locations from Rangers' 3-0 victory against Hibs at Easter Road in late December 2019. As you can see, Rangers' new shape was effectively a 2-3-4-1 in possession with the full-backs regularly making more of their passes in the opposition's half of the field. They played almost as orthodox wingers to utilise the space left by the wide attackers moving into more central areas of the pitch.

The central midfield three continued to evolve, with Ryan Jack, Steven Davis and Glen Kamara playing regularly together as a flat midfield three for the majority of this season.

The arrival of Filip Helander and the transformation in Borna Barišić also provided Rangers with something they had lacked hugely in the season prior – two left-footed defenders capable of building play from deep and contributing in the final third.

As a direct result, both full-backs could now perform similar roles, being responsible for providing the width and balance in the attack. In contrast, the wide forwards now started slightly

HIBERNIAN 0-3 RANGERS

SPFL Easter Road 20.12.19

The average pass locations from Rangers' 3-0 win against Hibernian in December 2019 show the team's attacking shape evolving into a 2-3-4-1 in possession.

FIGURE 21

deeper and were tasked with dropping into the half-spaces to try and exploit space. The full-backs could still rampage forward at will in support due to the extra cover provided by a wider, flatter central midfield.

COVID

Gerrard told Rangers TV, 'I'm very disappointed with the performance, frustrated with it. It doesn't give a true reflection of me, my staff, or our supporters. We got what we deserved today; we were second best from start to finish. Nowhere near creative enough, and they could have scored more goals against us. A quarter-final match with so much at stake; I'm so surprised at the performance we were given.

'This is the lowest I've felt since we walked in. It reminded me of some of the performances I had seen before I came in, and I'm responsible for that. I'm bitterly disappointed that after two years we played like in a quarter-final. For me to get that across the park today I'm feeling really disappointed. It's tough to lift the players, that's what I've been doing of late. We've given these players everything to help them on and off the pitch. If that's the performance level after two years of what we've gave them I should be very, very concerned.'

As the world began to shut down in March 2020 due to the COVID-19 pandemic, Gerrard was not happy and Rangers were in tactical turmoil once more. Injuries to key players and a loss of form across the squad had contributed to their poor performances in early January immediately following the winter break. As mentioned in the previous chapter, the first 19 league games had yielded a stunning 53 points out of 60 available, but in the remaining nine matches of a truncated season, Rangers would only pick up a further 13 points out of 30 to leave themselves 13 points behind Celtic, albeit with a game in hand. Rangers had also just been dumped out of the Scottish Cup at an early stage once again, this time at Tynecastle, losing 1-0 to bottom side Hearts on 29 February 2020, sparking the manager's comments on Rangers TV.

The 5-5 game against Hibs at Easter Road in May 2018 signalled the end of the previous era and the beginning of a new one. How close was this defeat to their Edinburgh rivals to being the end of the Gerrard era not even two years later? Thankfully, that's not a question we'll ever know the answer to, but those immediate post-match comments showed a man visibly in pain as he stared down a second trophyless season.

Some 142 days would pass between Rangers' final game of 2019/20 against Bayer Leverkusen and their first of 2020/21 against Aberdeen on 1 August. It was the longest period without a Rangers game since the war era as the club – along with most of the general population – went into a prolonged period of lockdown at the request of the government in the fight to limit the spread of COVID-19.

In an acrimonious vote on 10 April 2020, the member clubs of the Scottish Professional Football League voted in favour of abandoning the season with the current standings to be deemed as final placings with Rangers having nine games left to play.

Despite the circumstances surrounding the decision, Rangers' football department would use the enforced downtime to significant benefit. The work done in the spring period of 2020 represented the crucial final building blocks in the three-year pursuit of title glory.

'When the first lockdown happened and we realised that there was going to be a postponement, we didn't really know what we had to do, how long would we be in lockdown, was the season going to restart again. So we had to make a few plans that were different dependent upon the state of the actual virus,' Dr Mark Waller, the club's first-team doctor, said on the Relentle55 video.

Around this time, Rangers signed a partnership with Zone 7, a data-driven company that uses artificial intelligence to assist football clubs with preventing injuries. They do this by helping to calculate the peak training load and recovery each player requires to operate at their maximum. As a result of the delayed start to the season, the fixture schedule was packed throughout the campaign's first half, and there was simply not enough time for players to recover appropriately between games.

Speaking to Forbes.com, Tal Brown, Zone7's co-founder and chief executive said, 'Rangers had a 40 per cent reduction in injury rates this season. Can we take credit for their technical success? Absolutely not. But the fact is, they've got more available in their squad than anyone else they're competing with.'

The artificial intelligence system analyses vast volumes of data and provides detailed information taken straight from real-time data that would require Rangers to employ a significantly enhanced medical and analytics department should they wish to replicate this in-house. As Brown said, by the halfway stage in the season, Rangers had reported considerably fewer injuries than in the prior season.

As pre-season progressed, it became noticeable throughout the early games that certain players such as Joe Aribo and Glen Kamara had 'bulked up' due to the additional focus on gym work and the change in their fitness regime as a result of the break from playing competitive football. This, in addition to the work done in conjunction with Zone 7, undoubtedly had an enormous benefit on Rangers' durability in the early months of the season.

Gerrard said on Relentle55, 'The frustration of how the season before ended, the frustration of coronavirus and being in lockdown gave us an opportunity to reset. We could have talks with the players individually and collectively, we could reset as a staff and really focus on the 12 months coming up. It was a slow pre-season in terms of getting the boys back into rhythm and into the sessions but definitely the frustration of the previous season and a real long solid pre-season gave us a chance to reset and focus on our targets.'

Sporting director Ross Wilson added, 'As a club we saw it as an opportunity to prepare, plan and also review where have we been, how do we move forward. We had to try and plan as best as we could while understanding that a lot of things were out of our control.'

Most footballers around this period used Strava – an exercise tracking app – to time their daily runs and would often post their results on social media, some with amusingly artificial times. Rangers' fitness staff also used Strava to ensure players kept their fitness to the necessary levels and adopted other remote learning tools such as Zoom. These were provided to players in the same way as the general public to ensure the club could stay in contact during periods of isolation.

Speaking on *Relentle55: The Inside Story*, the video released to celebrate the club's title success, Steven Davis discussed how the players and coaching staff could communicate ideas and focus on areas of improvement both individually and as a team during these Zoom calls. Ianis Hagi is also on record as stating that he believes that the club's individual training programmes helped the players focus and improve themselves throughout this period despite the inability to train in the way they usually did.

Due to the ongoing COVID restrictions at the time, when pre-season training began in mid-June, it was on the basis that only small groups could train together to start with. Michael Beale has spoken previously about Tom Culshaw primarily working with the defenders in previous seasons, Gary McAllister and Steven Gerrard focusing on the midfielders and Beale himself usually coaching the forwards. Due to the restrictions, the coaching team changed their approach and instead took three different sessions each day, allowing them the time and space to work in detail with each section of the team and with specific individuals.

In the first two seasons under Gerrard, Rangers would effectively supplement their pre-season schedule with the early rounds of Europa League qualification, which accelerated their fitness and tactical awareness given the competitive nature of the ties. With the remaining matches of the Champions League and Europa League games from 2019/20 taking place throughout August, the upcoming season's qualifiers were delayed for two months to allow these to be completed. This meant that for the first time since their return to the top flight in 2016, Rangers had seven uninterrupted weeks of pre-season between training resuming on 15 June and their first competitive game of the season on 1 August.

There was no magic formula throughout this pre-season, as there hasn't been throughout the three years since Gerrard took charge. The importance of marginal gains is vastly underplayed in football and from that first game of the season at Pittodrie, the benefit of incremental improvements to an already well-oiled tactical structure would be clear for all to see as Rangers set about taking the league by storm.

2020 Squad Overview

Summer 2020 saw the completion of the final iteration of Rangers' squad rebuild and tactical evolution which ultimately ended in the unbeaten championship-winning season of 2020/21. After the unusually long COVID shutdown and long pre-season, it would be almost five months between the 3-1 defeat to Leverkusen in March 2020 and their first game of the new season, a 1-0 victory in early August away to Aberdeen courtesy of a first-half Ryan Kent goal.

The start to this season was personified by Rangers' outstanding clean sheet record as the defence remained unbreached until matchday eight, a breathless end-to-end 2-2 draw at Easter Road against Hibernian. The critical games throughout the league campaign will be explored in more detail later, but suffice to say that Rangers were thoroughly dominant from the moment they reached the top of the table at the end of matchday three until they became champions on 7 March, the first time a team had ever won the league that early. They would end up claiming 102 points from a possible 114, conceding just 13 goals in the process.

It's easy to forget, given that the club finished 25 points ahead of Celtic, but as the two sides squared up in the second Old Firm game of the season at Parkhead in October, Rangers were just one point clear having played a game more. Rangers annihilated Celtic that day in a performance that exuded supreme control, winning 2-0 courtesy of a double by Connor Goldson. All over the pitch, the team looked at the peak of their powers and from that moment on never looked back. Rangers would remain undefeated in all five games against Celtic in this season, winning four and drawing one, 1-1 in mid-March immediately after being crowned champions. It was a show of dominance that summed up both clubs' league campaigns.

In Europe, the journey was different to the previous two years. Rangers played the second leg of their Europa League last-16 tie against Leverkusen, going down 1-0 and exiting the previous season's tournament just a few days after the domestic season started. Indeed, due to COVID, Rangers' 2019/20 European campaign spanned an incredible 13 months and 395 days. With this unprecedented delay to proceedings, the qualification phase for 2020/21 would consist of one-legged ties played throughout September. Rangers dispatched Lincoln Red Imps and Willem II in Gibraltar and Holland respectively, before a particularly impressive 2-1 victory at Ibrox against Galatasaray sealed their place in the group stages for a third year in a row. Rangers would again successfully navigate their group, finishing unbeaten and at the top ahead of Benfica, Standard Liege and Lech Poznań.

Remarkably, Rangers led Portuguese giants Benfica by two goals in the 75th minute of both home and away ties and somehow contrived to concede four late goals to draw both games. Regardless, their performances in Europe this season were a remarkable achievement, particularly when you consider that starting point against FK Shkupi in July 2018. Rangers would demolish Royal Antwerp 9-5 on aggregate in the round of 32 with a devastating display of counter-attacking football by Ryan Kent and Alfredo Morelos in particular. In the last 16 they would fall short against Slavia Prague, losing 3-1 on aggregate and exiting the competition at the same stage as the season prior.

Again – and at danger of constantly repeating myself – the financial windfall that three Europa League Group stage qualifications in a row brought cannot be understated. The

Rangers board backed the football operations even with the unexpected – and probably still fully unrealised – blow to finances as a result of the COVID shutdown and with no idea when ticket sales and much-needed matchday revenues would start to return to normal. It has to be said that the Rangers fans more than played their part here too, selling out season tickets, purchasing some 30,000 My Gers subscriptions and clearing the shelves (virtual or otherwise) of every club-affiliated piece of merchandise they could lay their hands on. This backing by the board and fans was hugely important and was shown by the club signing players who would play major roles in helping the team qualify for the group stages and in the title charge.

When Ianis Hagi joined in January on an initial six-month loan, new sporting director Ross Wilson remarked that the deal included an option to purchase the player in the summer. The rumoured figure at that time was circa £4m and despite Rangers' poor form, Hagi had performed very well individually and most fans were in favour of the young Romanian signing permanently. In late May 2020, Rangers did just that with Hagi joining for a re-negotiated fee of around £3m, which was heralded as excellent work in the transfer market. Rangers acted swiftly and decisively to secure the talented 21-year-old amid interest from other clubs.

Hagi would enjoy an impressive first full season at Ibrox. Despite not always being a regular in the team, he would often pop up at crucial moments to change games with his innate and seemingly hereditary knack of finding team-mates in scoring positions.

He made 46 appearances in all competitions, with 13 of these coming from the bench as he finished the season with eight goals and 12 assists, the most of any Rangers player. His 11 assists in the league were also the highest in the SPFL, capping off a wonderful full debut season.

The general opinion was that Hagi was incredibly useful in domestic situations as a classic number ten who could assist

Rangers with breaking down opposition teams, something they had struggled with in the past. Interestingly though, he also started eight of the Europa League games with his underrated ability off the ball coming to the fore in bigger matches.

A few weeks after the signing of Hagi, Rangers would again utilise the cross-border loophole to sign Leicester City defender Calvin Bassey on a pre-contract agreement. Capable of playing at left-back and at centre-back, Bassey would add depth to an area of the pitch that needed it, with Borna Barišić the only recognised left-back remaining at the club. It would be a mixed debut campaign for Bassey with some excellent performances – most notably his rampaging display in the pouring rain in the 2-0 victory against Standard Liege in Belgium. At just 20 years of age, this signing was clearly one for the future, but these positive showings were peppered with some which showed he still had progress to make. One such example would be the disappointing League Cup quarter-final defeat to St Mirren in late December which would be his last appearance of the season.

Ross Wilson's impact on Rangers' transfer dealings again came to the fore when Croatian centre-back Niko Katić suffered a cruciate ligament injury in mid-July, just two weeks before the season started. With Filip Helander himself having returned from almost eight months out injured – an unfortunately all too recurring theme for the big Swede – the options to partner Connor Goldson were thin on the ground. Within a week of Katić's injury, Rangers had moved to snap up 32-year-old Nigerian international defender Leon Balogun on a free transfer following the expiration of his short-term contract at Wigan. Born in Germany, Balogun had spent the last four years playing in England with Brighton and Wigan Athletic but hadn't managed to get the regular game time that he clearly craved at his age.

Balogun would make his debut in the Aberdeen game and put in a performance that would go on to be his trademark throughout the season. Comfortable and assured in possession allied with a not insignificant turn of pace for a player of his age, the introduction of Balogun allowed Rangers' defensive line to play higher up the pitch and squeeze the opposition further into their own half. He would also be asked to fill in at right-back due to injuries and illness, and while not a role that appears best suited to his skillset, he had played there in the past and was more than happy to help the team as and when required.

Another 32-year-old joining on a free transfer was Scotland international goalkeeper Jon McLaughlin to replace Sheffield United-bound Wes Foderingham, who left after failing to regain his number one jersey in Gerrard's first two seasons. McLaughlin would push McGregor to new levels in 2020/21, making more appearances than he might have expected in the early months. In total, he finished the season with 14 appearances and an incredible 12 clean sheets as he provided a much-needed rotation option to his 39-year-old team-mate.

Following his 18-month loan spell, Jermain Defoe elected to sign on a one-year deal to continue his role as backup to number one striker Alfredo Morelos. Throughout Defoe's two and a half years at Ibrox, his goalscoring ability has shown no sign of waning, with the Englishman netting 35 times in just 72 appearances.

Morelos had been heavily rumoured to leave Rangers in every transfer window since he joined and summer 2020 was no different, irrespective of the pandemic. It was the turn of French side Lille – who would go on to become Ligue 1 champions in 2020/21 – this time, and with rumours of bids of upwards of £15m being rebuffed as Rangers seemed determined to hold out for top dollar for any asset, it seemed only a matter of time before he would depart.

With that prospect assumedly in mind, Rangers moved to bring in two forwards on the same day with a few weeks remaining in the transfer window. Anderlecht forward Kemar Roofe, 27, joined, as did 23-year-old Swiss striker Cedric Itten from St Gallen. Roofe was a serious statement of intent from

Rangers, a player they had been rumoured to be tracking the year before his move from Leeds to Belgium. Roofe had been a key player in his three years at Elland Road, particularly in his final season, the first under the tutelage of Marcelo Bielsa. With just one season remaining on his contract, Leeds elected to cash in on Roofe and the player himself revealed a long-term desire to play in Europe and felt that Anderlecht represented the best chance of doing so and duly signed for the Belgian club for approximately £7m.

While undoubtedly an extremely talented player, Roofe is long known as suffering from recurring injuries and hadn't played for Anderlecht since January 2020. It's a very Rangers decision to sign a player with injury problems and not get value for money, but despite suffering injuries during this season, the club did manage to eke out enough value from the Jamaican international as he finished the season with 19 goals to be the club's top scorer. The transfer fee Rangers paid was not released, but it was rumoured at the time that Ross Wilson had again secured a discount on the player with sums of approximately £3m to £4m being mooted. Having someone to share the burden with Morelos, who did remain at Ibrox after all, proved vital as the season progressed.

With Roofe and Morelos ahead of him in the queue, chances to make an impression were few and far between for Cedric Itten. He had scored 19 goals in 34 appearances for St Gallen in the previous season; however, their style appeared to be at odds with the way Rangers played. A large percentage of those goals came from wide attackers crossing into the box, and Itten playing off of a strike partner in a 4-4-2 formation. Given Morelos ended up staying with Rangers, and the superior technical ability that Roofe possessed, Itten was unfortunately reduced to an alternative option off the bench. He played his part, though, particularly in a nervy league victory in mid-December. Rangers had crashed out of the League Cup a few days before and were losing to Motherwell at Ibrox with just

17 minutes remaining. Roofe's goal and an Itten double saved Christmas 2020 and ensured Rangers could continue their near-perfect league form at a tricky time of year, particularly bearing in mind the struggles they had faced during January in both of the previous two seasons.

Eternal loanees Jason Holt, Jordan Rossiter and Jak Alnwick eventually left on free transfers, as did Jordan Jones and Ross McCrorie on loan. The latter pair joined Sunderland and Aberdeen respectively. In McCrorie's case, there was a slight surprise when Rangers included an agreed option to buy in McCrorie's deal for summer 2021, but it was clear that the standard of players at the club had progressed to such a level that there would be limited game time available for a player like him moving forward.

Three others also departed and feelings were also mixed at this news for various reasons. In his first two years at Ibrox, Andy Halliday had proved to be a valuable squad player under Gerrard, most noticeably with an outstanding performance in that marker-setting first Old Firm win in December 2018. Gerrard called Halliday his 'unofficial captain' in the aftermath of this game, and as a Rangers die-hard, his passion for the club never failed to shine through. Greg Docherty had joined six months before Gerrard joined and always appeared to show up well in training, particularly impressing with his incredible fitness. Clearly, the management team felt he wasn't at the technical level to stake a claim for the first-team squad on an ongoing basis, and he departed to Hull on a permanent deal. Another who joined in that last pre-Gerrard transfer window was Jamie Murphy, who played regularly in the early games of the Liverpudlian's tenure but suffered the cruellest of blows, a cruciate ligament injury against Kilmarnock in just his eighth appearance of the season. Murphy was a talented player with a very keen eye for goal, having played successfully in the upper reaches of the English Championship for several years. Still, sadly upon his return from injury, he couldn't quite get himself back up to the level required to play a key role in the team. He enjoyed a successful loan spell at Burton Albion, which was cut short due to the pandemic, and eventually joined Hibernian on a loan deal with an option to go permanent at the end of 2020/21.

In the January transfer window, 23-year-old Aberdeen forward Scott Wright and 24-year-old centre-half Jack Simpson were signed on pre-contracts awhich were then made permanent before the end of the window. Both would treat the first six months of their career as settling-in periods, with Wright in particular making a decent impression throughout the second half of the title-winning campaign as a ball-carrying left-winger.

The key word for Rangers under Gerrard has always been evolution, whether it be increasing the quality of players available, improving the players already at the club or implementing the tactical philosophy. Rangers' tactical shape under Gerrard has evolved considerably in the last three years in terms of structure and player quality. While it is, in essence, composed of a four-man defence with three central midfielders and three forwards, it's pertinent to note that there can be a marked difference between a player's position on the pitch and his tactical role within the structure of the team.

With the acquisition of Leon Balogun, Rangers were able to press higher and reduce the space between the defence and midfield much more effectively than they could with players less comfortable in possession.

Rangers' full-backs were the primary creative outlets within the team, regularly impacting the final third and creating many chances for their team-mates (and on occasion, each other). On several occasions in 2020/21, Rangers varied the starting positions of the full-backs depending on the opposition. When faced with a five-man defence, they would at times withdraw them ten yards and attempt to draw the opposition out to create spaces in behind. In others, one full-back would sit back and allow the other to attack in a more classic relationship. Still, in most games, they would continue to adopt their now-familiar high, aggressive position in the opposition's half when Rangers were in possession.

On occasions where Rangers are not expected to dominate possession or depending on the in-game situation, one of the number eights was withdrawn alongside the number six to create a double pivot. This has the added benefit of providing additional defensive cover in central areas but also allows the second number eight to advance forward into the number ten role, effectively creating a 4-2-3-1 formation in possession. Rangers can also elect to revert back to their flat midfield three shape when the challenge requires it, as seen in the 3-3 draw away to Benfica in this season.

Figure 22

Similarly, in games where Rangers are expected to have large amounts of possession, they introduced two attacking number eights to central midfield to allow the team to dominate fully in the centre of the pitch and suffocate the opposition with central running and line-breaking passes.

The introduction of another goalscorer to the forward line in the shape of Kemar Roofe added a significant additional threat to the team in the attacking area of the pitch. In that previous season, Nigerian box-to-box midfielder Joe Aribo played the majority of games on the right of the attack, with Daniel Candeias, a journeyman classic winger, doing similar in the first season. By listing these three players, you can clearly see how the impact of a specific tactical role on the pitch can be transformed simply by selecting a player with a different skillset.

On paper, Morelos, Roofe and Ryan Kent have a combination of skills that complement each other and while they did not play as many games together as the manager would have liked, all three played significant roles in the title victory. Kent started the season in explosive fashion, with big increases in his goals and shot volume from the year before. In the autumn and early

MIDFIELD FLEXIBILITY

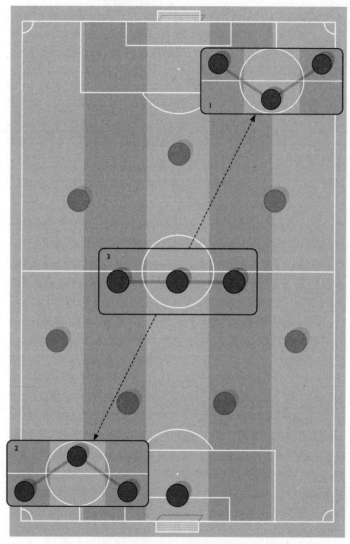

Rangers' midfield flexibility allowed them to switch between a single pivot, double pivot and a flat midfield three regularly, sometimes within the same game.

FIGURE 22

winter months, Roofe took up the attacking mantle, and his goals were crucial in taking the team through to the end of the year. Neatly, Morelos would then take his turn and score vital goals in huge domestic away games throughout January and February to seal the title.

There are stars in all areas of the pitch, but the story of this championship season is the team working together as a unit with key players taking their turn at critical moments to deliver.

In the final Old Firm match up of season 2020/21, Rangers again showed their tactical flexibility by debuting a new 4-3-1-2 shape with Ryan Kent playing as a number ten behind Roofe and Morelos. The switch caused havoc in a beleaguered Celtic side and Kent's performance allied to the convincing win gave a potential glimpse into the next tactical evolution of this team.

Figure 23

RANGERS 4 - 1 CELTIC
SPFL Ibrox Stadium 02.05.20

Rangers debuted a 4-3-1-2 formation in the final Old Firm game of the
Championship-winning season.

FIGURE 23

3

Player and Tactical Role Evolution

Goalkeeper

'It was just one of these things – you react to it, you see it, you stick your hand out and hopefully it doesn't go in. And it didn't, so happy days.'

Allan McGregor, Glasgow Times, *March 2021*

The position of goalkeeper could be described as unloved when discussing football tactics. Formations listed on the page do not even include the goalkeeper, albeit it is more common on the continent to include them such as a 1-4-2-3-1 formation. The point remains that it is not standard practice.

The goalkeeping position was changed forever in 1992 with the introduction of the back-pass rule, meaning that a goalkeeper was now forbidden from handling the ball when passed to them by their own team-mate. This change meant that a goalkeeper's skillset had to evolve to be more comfortable with the ball at his feet, albeit it was a slower process than some may have envisioned. Until the 2010s and the emergence of players such as Manuel Neuer at Bayern Munich and Ederson at Manchester City, a goalkeeper who was just as comfortable in possession as he was at shot-stopping was still the exception rather than the rule. These two players illustrate how important a goalkeeper can be when in possession and how their role has changed, with both playing key roles in building attacks from deep and also acting as de facto sweepers, rushing out of goal to snuff out potential opposition counter-attacks.

Rangers have been truly blessed in my lifetime with legendary goalkeepers all the way from England international Chris Woods, through to the greatest ever in Andy Goram, right up to Allan McGregor, who first signed for Rangers as a schoolboy in 1998, just as The Goalie called time on his Rangers career.

McGregor made his debut for Rangers in a cup tie against Forfar in February 2002, and following two successful loan spells became the club's undisputed first choice between 2006 and 2012. He would take the gloves again from Wes Foderingham when he re-signed in 2018 at the grand old age of 36.

The tactical role of the goalkeeper in Gerrard's team remained consistent throughout the three seasons. On the whole, their primary function is as a more traditional shot-stopper. While McGregor has never been terrible in possession of the ball, it's fair to say that his strengths lay predominantly in the more traditional sphere of goalkeeping, specifically in his outstanding shot-stopping ability. Similarly, McGregor has never been a goalkeeper who commands his box in the air, often preferring to stay on his line rather than deal with crosses and instead gamble on his reactions should he then be faced with a shot.

That's not to do McGregor a disservice; he is an outstanding goalkeeper, one of the very best in the club's history, and will quite rightly be regarded as a club legend. Throughout his second spell at Ibrox he played just as big a part as any other Ranger and his vast array of outstanding saves – none more so than that breathtaking 'Happy Days' save against Slavia Prague – will be remembered for decades to come. In the dying minutes of the aforementioned game, he incredibly clawed the ball one-handed off his line to keep Rangers in their last-16 tie.

McGregor's saves are as much part of this story as Tavernier's assists or Morelos's goals. Every so often, players come along who transcend tactical shapes or philosophies, and McGregor was of the quality that this deserves to apply to him also.

As mentioned, the role of a goalkeeper has evolved significantly throughout the latter half of McGregor's 20-year career. As he turned 39 during the title-winning season it's unrealistic to expect him to ever be as comfortable with the ball at his feet as younger goalkeepers will be, but he still proved to be an asset on the ball. During Rangers' build-up play, McGregor was used mostly to restart attacks with short passes into the centre-backs, who would then in turn look to distribute the ball through the middle of the pitch or out to the full-backs. On the admittedly rare occasions that Rangers were pressed high up the pitch by an opposition team, McGregor did look to bypass this press and play mid-range passes into the head of either full-back thus allowing the team to continue to build attacks through their preferred routes.

Figure 24

In Jon McLaughlin, Rangers had a backup who was much more comfortable in possession and would regularly look to draw the opposition attackers forward to try to create gaps in their pressure before attempting riskier passes. In some ways, McLaughlin was a more modern goalkeeper and could be classed as the opposite of McGregor stylistically, with the latter also famed for his reluctance to leave his line for crosses and preferring to rely on his shot-stopping ability should the opposition attackers make first contact with the ball.

There were pros and cons of both players' styles but it was generally accepted that they complemented each other well as number one and number two. What was also not in doubt was that both played vital roles in Rangers' season, as evidenced by the 26 combined clean sheets they racked up in the league, breaking yet another SPFL record.

MCGREGOR'S DISTRIBUTION

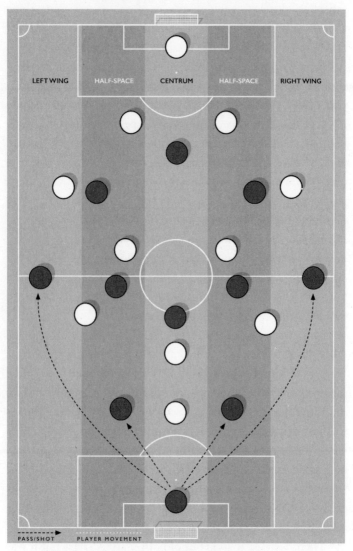

McGregor's contribution in build-up was mostly limited to recycling possession, but on occasion
he would begin attacks with mid-range passes into the full-backs.

FIGURE 24

Centre-Backs

'He naturally gives us balance as a left-footer. That enables us to play with a two or with a back three. He will be able to defend our box and be a threat at set pieces. He is comfortable on the ball. He's a good man, he's a leader.'

Steven Gerrard on Filip Helander, Scottish Sun, *August 2019*

Jock 'Tiger' Shaw, Davie Meiklejohn, Terry Butcher, Richard Gough, Lorenzo Amoruso, Davie Weir. Throughout Rangers' history the club has been blessed with a fantastic array of central defenders. Each one brought differing attributes but all were undeniably the leaders of the defence, if not the entire team. In the great teams of years gone past, the centre-back position was very much as you would expect, defend first and ask questions later.

As football evolved throughout the latter half of the the 20th century, so too did the requirements for this role. Richard Gough was my first Rangers captain, being appointed to this role two days before my fifth birthday and several years prior to my first season ticket in 1994. Growing up, he was THE Rangers captain to me and many of my generation. A leader on and off the pitch, a terrific defender and more than capable of popping up with a goal in the opposition box – something which always seems to help grow an affinity with a centre-back.

Players such as ex-England captain Terry Butcher were not only inspirational captains, they were capable of dominating any centre-forward who dared cross their path, and they could also play a bit too.

Rangers used ball-playing centre-backs before this term really entered the Scottish footballing lexicon. Butcher and Amoruso were more than comfortable in possession, albeit the latter possibly thought he was more comfortable than he was, as anyone present at Ibrox in the November 2000 loss to Monaco in the Champions League might confirm. Even into the more modern era, to this day, Algerian Madjid Bougherra – who played for the club for three seasons during Walter Smith's second spell as manager – is one of the most technical players in a true footballing sense to have appeared at centre-back in the famous blue shirt.

The role has changed so much over the years that it can be challenging to pinpoint the specific skillset required of the position in the modern game. Many coaches or scouts will invariably tell you that analysis and scouting for a centre-back is a notoriously tricky task. There are a few reasons why, but the main issue centres on the fact that completely different requirements are placed upon centre-backs depending on the specific team they play for. For example, a centre-back playing for a team like Burnley will see limited amounts of the ball due to their team's more direct playing style and status within their respective league. A Burnley centre-back can also expect to spend more time actively engaged in the art of traditional defending than, say, one playing for Manchester City. Ordinarily, they would be required to play a key role in possession and, as such, would need to be comfortable doing so. To that end, both teams will have completely different centre-back profiles that they would look to recruit, and the type of players who will be selected won't tend to deviate from these game to game as much as other positions might.

In terms of data analysis, there are also more definitive metrics for midfielders and attackers. Passes, key passes, expected assists, expected goals and shots on target all help to paint a picture of the type of player from a creative point of view. For defenders, it's a lot more nuanced. Has the player won ten tackles in a game because this is a key strength of his? Or is his positioning suspect, or perhaps he lacks pace, and it's a last-ditch slide tackle? Does he not win as many headers as another centre-back because he's poor in the air, or is he playing in a more attacking, ball-focused team and involved less?

A centre-back's primary job in any team is stopping players shooting on target from in and around the 18-yard box. Statistics also now exist that show which chances are given away from which centre-back's zone of influence; i.e., does the chance originate from the left or the right side of central defence? Again, it's not an exact science, but you can at least see from which area of the pitch shots are being conceded and delve deeper into the potential reasons for this.

With the evolution of the role, the desired skillset for a centre-back has undertaken a radical change during the 21st century. Gone are those days where a centre-back could get away with defending first, with the sole focus of taking man, ball and sometimes corner flag in the pursuit of a clean sheet. In the ever-elusive quest to find more space to manipulate a team's advantage on the pitch, centre-backs are now required to play a much more integral role on the ball, particularly in building attacks.

To that end and as introduced earlier, Rangers essentially adopted a 2-3-4-1 when in possession throughout the latter period under Steven Gerrard's management. With such attacking full-backs, the onus was on both centre-backs to be competent one vs one defenders, to be excellent in possession and also be capable of building play from the back. For example, it was not uncommon for Connor Goldson to make upwards of

70 passes on average per game and over the three years under Gerrard, his passing range would become a crucial tool in Rangers' attacking arsenal.

Around 10 to 15 years ago, most modern centre-back pairings would consist of a ball-player partnered with a more traditional ball-winning stopper. The ball-player would be tasked with initiating attacks and building play from deep, but not to anywhere near the extent that we see modern centre-backs doing today. In contrast, the stopper was primarily concerned with stopping the ball from going past the goalkeeper by any means possible. In most situations, this type of pairing is probably still the case, although the 'stopper' role is becoming less prevalent such is that overwhelming need for defenders to be more all-round footballers.

With an average of 63 per cent possession in league games in 2020/21, two aggressive, physical centre-backs who were comfortable on the ball and capable of building attacks were vital to the way Rangers played. The partnership between Goldson and Filip Helander or Goldson and Leon Balogun was pretty standard; all three were comfortable on the ball and Rangers would tend to utilise one player more than others (usually Goldson) when attempting to build play from the back. This was done either through passing or by carrying the ball into midfield to initiate the defending team's line of pressure. The other centre-back would act as a covering player, tasked with sweeping up behind in the event of any counter-attacks from the opposition.

Goldson was a virtual ever-present over Gerrard's first three years, racking up an incredible 162 appearances from a possible 170 in all competitions. This remarkable achievement includes playing every single minute of every single game as Rangers rampaged to their 55th Scottish Premiership title and enjoyed a deep run to the last 16 of the Europa League.

Throughout these three seasons, Goldson's defensive partner changed regularly due to a combination of factors.

During 2018/19, Niko Katić was Goldson's most regular partner, and having both joined the club that summer the two forged an excellent understanding in a remarkably short space of time. In the European qualifying games, in particular, both were outstanding, but none more so than in the 1-1 draw away to Russian Premier League outfit Ufa in the Europa League play-off round. Having won the first leg 1-0 at Ibrox, Rangers travelled deep into Russia in search of the draw that would ensure their safe passage through to the group stage. As ever with Rangers, things didn't go to plan as the team ended up playing for an hour with ten men and 25 minutes with just nine. Given they had played just 11 competitive games together before this night, both Goldson and Katić were outstanding and played a huge part in Rangers seeing out that match. This win resulted in the team gaining entry to the Europa League – a colossal achievement for Gerrard and Rangers so early in that first season.

In the early months, Rangers usually built up their attacks with the two centre-backs and three midfielders in front as shown in earlier chapters, which ensured plenty of options when playing out from the back. Goldson almost always played as the right-sided centre-back, and would take on the role of the covering player, with Katić playing on the left as the more aggressive, tasked with winning the ball in the air. Goldson's use of the ball and ability to build play from deep meant this was a natural partnership and was considered a success throughout this debut season.

Given a choice, both centre-backs elected to go short and play angled passes into the number six, usually Ross McCrorie. As McCrorie was a centre-back by trade, his ability to receive these passes and begin attacking moves wasn't at the level required at this stage of his development. Another option for building attacks was to utilise the full-backs, and look to attack down the sides of the opposition which gave the centre-backs multiple short options and hindered the opposition from closing down effectively. More risky line-breaking passes through to the attacking players were seldom seen in the earlier months, as this relied on both centre-backs including variation in their passing range when faced with forwards, which was not always the case.

Katić was an outstanding siege defender and capable of dominating most centre-forwards physically despite his relatively tender age, but it's fair to say he was not as adept with the ball at his feet as Goldson. With the further complication of Katić being right-footed yet playing on the left, he was regularly identified as a potential weakness in Rangers' set-up. In certain situations, teams would recognise this issue and target Katić's discomfort on the ball either by leaving him in possession and blocking off passing lanes or by identifying him as their 'pressing victim' to attempt to win the ball back high up the pitch.

Figure 25

In the 2-0 defeat to Celtic at Ibrox in early September 2019, Celtic arrived with a clear plan to disrupt Rangers' defence and they executed this with great success. Their strategy on this occasion was predicated on leaving Katić in possession and retreating into their defensive structure while blocking all passing angles. This left Katić with no other choice than to either recycle possession straight back to Glen Kamara, carry the ball forward from deep himself or turn back and retreat as he does in this situation. Due to Celtic's pressing, Katić was eventually forced to play the ball back to Allan McGregor with limited passing options available. McGregor then had to play a riskier long ball, resulting in Rangers turning over possession deep in Celtic's half.

Where possible, Gerrard elected to play to Katić's strengths and allowed him to be the aggressive centre-back tasked with winning the ball back in the air and on the deck as quickly as possible. This strategy worked to positive effect for the most

KATIĆ IN POSSESSION
Rangers 0-2 Celtic SPFL 01.09.19

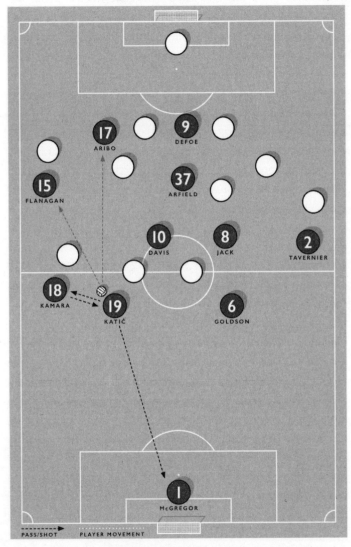

As a right-footed player playing as left centre-half, Katic struggled to play out from the back and was an easy target for opposition teams' pressing.

FIGURE 25

part, but in certain situations, Katić's desire to win the ball at all costs could prove to have a negative impact. Such was this keenness to dominate forwards physically, Katić would on occasion challenge for aerial balls he had little chance of winning, thus creating gaps in the team's defensive structure, resulting in chances being conceded. Katić was still a key member of the squad throughout his two full seasons playing regularly at the club and, at just 23 years old when the 2019/20 season ended, there was still time to learn and grow as a centre-back. When this aggression was appropriately channelled, the outcome could prove pivotal as it was with his dominant performance and match-winning header in Rangers' 2-1 victory at Parkhead in December 2019.

Figure 26

The arrival of 26-year-old Filip Helander in August 2019 provided Rangers with a much more experienced and rounded centre-back partner for Goldson. Not as aggressive as Katić in a physical match-up but an excellent reader of the game, Helander immediately impacted positively on the team. During his two full seasons at the club, Helander had still not been on the pitch during a domestic defeat for Rangers, spanning a total of 28 league games. It's an incredible statistic made all the more impressive when you consider he started the League Cup Final defeat to Celtic in December 2019 and the Scottish Cup quarter-final loss to St Johnstone in April 2021. He left both of these games early due to injury, and Rangers would go on to lose them by conceding goals from set pieces. It became clear that no Helander was fast becoming no party for Rangers, such was his understated influence on an already impressive defensive set-up. What is also apparent is that Helander only appeared in 30 of Rangers' 67 league games in that time period, as injuries proved an all too regular occurrence for the man from Malmö.

The signing of Helander clearly indicated that the management team had identified an opportunity to inject

HELANDER IN POSSESSION
Porto 1-1 Rangers Europa League 24.10.19

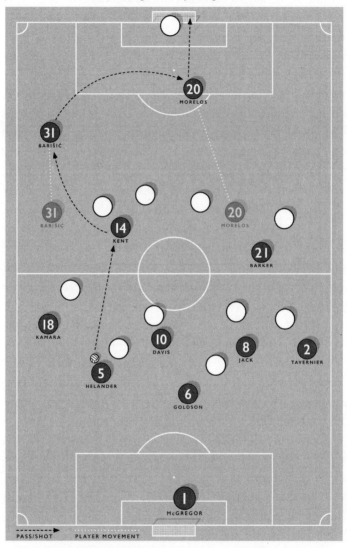

The introduction of left-footed Filip Helander coupled with the form of Borna Barišić ensured Rangers were able to build better attacks from the left and often score some memorable goals.

FIGURE 26

more flexibility and quality into the centre of their defence. Comfortable playing in a back three from his time in Serie A and crucially as a natural left-footer, Helander provided that balance to the defence that just wasn't possible with the right-footed Katić. With left-back Borna Barišić also being naturally left-footed, every build of play from that side had felt clunky and imperfect prior to the pair's arrival. Instantly, Helander was able to help open up that side of the defensive third and provide Rangers with another dimension and avenues to progress the ball quickly through the lines.

This was borne out later in the 2019/20 season and can be seen in the build-up to Alfredo Morelos's outstanding goal in the 1-1 draw with Porto in the Europa League group stages. From his position at left centre-back, Helander calmly received a pass from Goldson under pressure from the Porto forward line and the natural instinct is that he would look to turn back and play the safe pass back to McGregor in goal. Instead, Helander calmly let the ball roll across his body on to his stronger foot and played a first-time quick vertical pass straight through the midfield line of pressure and into the feet of Ryan Kent. A quick round the corner flicked pass from Kent found Barišić, who had advanced into plenty of space on the flank, and with yet another first he delivered an inch-perfect cross into Morelos who lashed home the equaliser from just inside the penalty area.

It was not the most difficult of passes for Helander, but equally not one that any other Rangers centre-back of the eight years previous (except for Goldson) would have been equipped to make. This signified a shift for Rangers offensively, but more important than his ability to progress the ball, Helander's positional sense and defensive ability provided a calming influence to the back four that would give the base as this team started to evolve into a dangerous attacking unit at European level.

Helander was missing from the team from early December 2019 due to injury, returning in the Europa League last 16 defeat to Bayer Leverkusen some eight months later following the COVID shutdown. His defensive prowess seemed even more pronounced throughout 2020/21 as he adapted his role tactically, becoming more of a covering centre-back than the aggressor he had been. His passing became slightly less adventurous than the season before, too, as Goldson would go on to evolve his pass selection to an unprecedented level.

Always better on the ball than given credit for, Connor Goldson was, however, also prone to the odd lapse in concentration. This is magnified as an Old Firm centre-half, given the sheer amount of possession these players enjoy. With opposition teams defending so deep, a risky pass is usually required to attempt to break through and should this go awry, the margin for error is pretty high.

That being said, there was a clear improvement in Goldson's overall passing over the seasons but in particular with his long-range balls. Instead of five-yard passes to James Tavernier or Steven Davis, which pushed the onus on to them to build play through tight midfield zones, Goldson would instead regularly 'miss out' a pass to a nearer team-mate. He would often elect to play longer, vertical passes into the forwards or advancing full-backs, allowing Rangers to break down teams much more efficiently. In turn, this allowed the midfield and full-backs to push slightly higher when the centre-backs were in possession, enabling them to stretch play and find pockets of space to attack in much more dangerous areas of the pitch.

If there is one pass that sums up the improvement, it is arguably the most crucial in a modern centre-back's attacking arsenal, the long diagonal switch of play.

Figure 27

As you can see in the example overleaf, in a League Cup tie against League One Falkirk in late 2020, Goldson strode forward with the ball scanning for a pass through the lines to build another attack against a deep-lying defence. The

GOLDSON'S LONG PASSING
Falkirk 0-4 Rangers Scottish League Cup 30.11.20

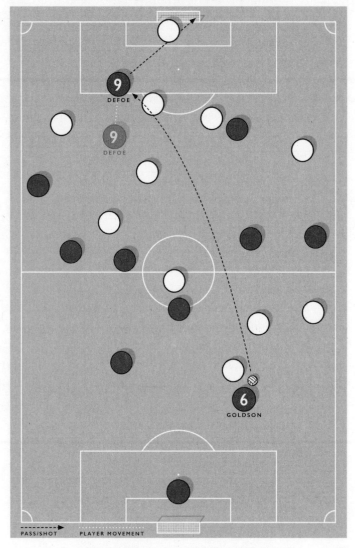

Connor Goldson's quality in possession evolved significantly over the three years,
particularly when passing over long distances.

FIGURE 27

midfield and full-backs have pushed high as detailed above to hem Falkirk into their defensive zone. Goldson takes a single touch to initiate pressure from Falkirk attacker Connor Sammon, which should create a passing angle for Rangers to progress upfield. Instead, Goldson caught Falkirk by surprise with a long raking pass to take advantage of a trademark Jermain Defoe run off the last defender. The execution of the pass was perfect, putting Defoe clean through on goal to score a very early opener and set Rangers on their way to a convincing victory.

It's this ability to carry the ball, initiate the first line of pressure and more importantly, have the vision to see and the skill to execute this risky pass that saw Goldson improve from a good all-round centre-back to the best in Scotland.

Figure 28

Leon Balogun joined Rangers on a free transfer in summer 2020 in what seemed like a last-minute signing solely due to an unfortunate cruciate ligament injury sustained by Niko Katić in pre-season. Balogun could be classed as much more of a modern centre-back than Helander or Katić as his skills were more pronounced in possession, preferring to defend high and aggressively and gamble on making good use of his recovery pace as and when required.

Having a player with a decent turn of pace in the back line improved Rangers again as this allowed the team to implement a risk and reward strategy to defending in certain games. This strategy served Rangers very well at Ibrox in 2020/21 as they were expected to dominate huge swathes of games and would have the vast majority of possession. The team were generally tasked with breaking down ultra-low blocks to the point it was not uncommon to face five-man defences plus four withdrawn midfielders and a sole striker. On one particular occasion, Motherwell came to Ibrox with a 5-5-0 formation, which gives an indication into some teams' attacking intent.

RANGERS' HIGH LINE

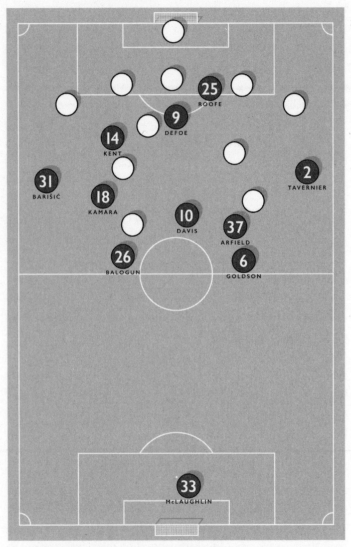

Using Leon Balogun's recovery pace, Rangers were able to utilise a very high line in matches at Ibrox.
This helped to hem opponents into their own defensive third and keep pressure on.

FIGURE 28

Having two centre-backs in Goldson and Balogun, who were very comfortable in possession, allowed Rangers to set their defensive line higher up the pitch and keep the pressure on the opposing team in a more focused, aggressive manner. This effectively allowed the team to create waves of attacks, hem the opponents into their own half, and attempt to force defensive mistakes to capitalise on.

To further illustrate the differing skillsets that Helander and Balogun offer, Helander attempted only three dribbles in 1,935 minutes of league football in 2020/21, whereas Balogun attempted 14 dribbles in just 1,415 minutes. Balogun's ability to carry the ball forward in possession also helped to commit the opposition's press and thus create gaps for the attacking players to exploit.

Making good use of Balogun's aforementioned recovery pace was also crucial in reducing any potential danger from counter-attacks. When their team-mates lost possession of the ball in the final third, Rangers were aggressive in preventing the pass into the striker's feet, often maintaining the pressure on the opposition by starting a new wave of attacks. Indeed, it was not uncommon for the entire Rangers team to be camped in the opposition half for the whole game, such was the team's dominance in possession and the coaching staff's intent to squeeze as much space as possible to hem opponents in.

While Balogun and Helander both offered varying skillsets alongside Goldson, having the flexibility to switch between the two players from game to game proved crucial.

In Goldson, Helander and Balogun, Rangers could call on three very impressive centre-backs during this title-winning campaign. That flexibility mentioned earlier, which coursed throughout the team, was evident once again despite each player's different skills, strengths and weaknesses. They were all able to complement each other perfectly throughout the campaign.

While defending is always a team game – particularly in a disciplined and highly structured side – the entire defensive unit deserves the utmost credit for the unprecedented levels they reached in 2020/21, particularly at Ibrox where that higher defensive line and intent to hem opponents into their own half saw the team win all 19 of their home league games, conceding a paltry four goals in the process.

Full-Back Playmakers

'I have played with some fantastic attacking right-backs – Kyle Walker, Glen Johnson, Steve Finnan to name a few. Tav is right up there. The way we play really suits James. The pleasing thing for me is he is still contributing to the other side of the game. He's pressing, he's really aggressive, he's winning his duels, stopping crosses.

'Our clean sheet record, to me, is just as important as James' other numbers. Where he is right now, he needs to bottle it and stay there for as long as he can because he's in fantastic form.'

Steven Gerrard on James Tavernier, rangers.co.uk,
December 2020

The full-back role within modern football has undergone a drastic transformation in the last 15 years. For a young Glasgow boy in the 1990s, an attacking full-back such as Cafu or Roberto Carlos felt like something from another universe, a mythical idea that only Brazil and their hypnotic samba flair could pull off. In 2008, another rampaging Brazilian full-back joined Barcelona at the start of an extraordinary period for the Spanish club and began revolutionising the role into what we now see as the gold standard.

Over the next few years, it was not outlandish to suggest that Dani Alves was the third-best player in the world behind team-mate Leo Messi and Real Madrid's Cristiano Ronaldo, as frequently suggested by *The Guardian*'s La Liga correspondent Sid Lowe. His cavalier approach to the role was a breath of fresh air and, when coupled with the inverted wing play of team-mate Pedro, was an essential facet of Pep Guardiola's all-conquering Barcelona team.

In buccaneering right-back and club captain James Tavernier, Rangers arguably had a player with a similar skillset and importance to their team as Barcelona did. Since his signing way back in June 2015, Tavernier was not only Rangers' current longest-serving player but he was also their most consistent playmaker year after year. Until Steven Gerrard joined and instantly made him captain, Tavernier was known as an ultra-attacking full-back with poor defensive capability, with a sizeable minority of fans preferring the more defensive-minded full-backs they had grown accustomed to over the many years previous. Each year under Gerrard, Tavernier's role continued to evolve and, with each adaptation, brought about another uptick in performance.

His role in 2020/21 could best be described as that of a full-back playmaker, with arguably only Liverpool's Trent Alexander-Arnold as his rival in terms of creative influence to his team from the full-back position. Tavernier contributed to the attack both on the overlap by whipping enticing balls into the box but equally on the underlap, engaging in quick combination play with midfielders and attackers. He would even take this one step further at periods during this season by driving into the box himself to finish moves off in a style akin to a more traditional attacking number eight.

To begin to describe this evolution, we also need to understand the starting point way back in Gerrard's first season as Rangers manager. In 2018/19, Tavernier and Portuguese winger Daniel Candeias formed a very good partnership on the right flank. Candeias – an all-action if not remarkably consistent traditional right-winger – had the pace, engine and positional awareness to either attack teams himself, or to provide intelligent cover for Tavernier's frequent forays forward. Both players would work well in tandem, taking turns to swing crosses into the box from various angles on the pitch. This was Rangers' primary source of attacking output in 2018/19, and the typical full-back and winger partnership characterised it, finishing with the pair combining for a total of 27 assists throughout this season.

It's a fallacy that Tavernier was very poor defensively as he can be strong one on one and was able to react well in defensive situations to intercept dangerous passes and restart attacks. Yes, he had his moments and gave the impression of being caught out of position, but as an ultra-attacking full-back in a dominant team, there has to be an element of risk versus reward to utilise him to his full attacking effect. Try as they might, modern-day full-backs cannot be in both places at once, and there will be certain situations within a game where a turnover of possession will happen, and they will be caught upfield. Without stunting the huge positives of his attacking play, it's essential to have a solid structure behind to cope with counter-attacks, scenarios in which Candeias's pace and defensive awareness proved crucial during this season.

When Candeias departed at the end of 2018/19, many were surprised as he was still a highly valued member of the squad, and it was thought that Tavernier would miss the protection he undoubtedly gave him. The coaching team seemed to agree, but rather than replace him like for like, Rangers would evolve another area of the team – the centre of midfield – in order to give Tavernier the support he required to play his natural game which he continued to do to impressive effect.

Figure 29

The synergy between Candeias and Tavernier was apparent from as early as the eighth minute of the very first game of Gerrard's management career against FK Shkupi in the first

TAVERNIER

THE AREAS OF THE PITCH THAT TAVERNIER CROSSED THE BALL FROM AND HOW HE ATTACKS

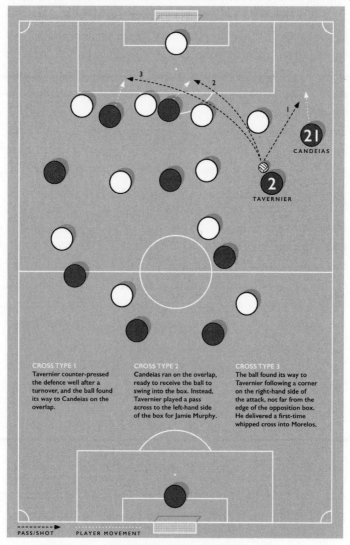

CROSS TYPE 1
Tavernier counter-pressed the defence well after a turnover, and the ball found its way to Candeias on the overlap.

CROSS TYPE 2
Candeias ran on the overlap, ready to receive the ball to swing into the box. Instead, Tavernier played a pass across to the left-hand side of the box for Jamie Murphy.

CROSS TYPE 3
The ball found its way to Tavernier following a corner on the right-hand side of the attack, not far from the edge of the opposition box. He delivered a first-time whipped cross into Morelos.

PASS/SHOT   PLAYER MOVEMENT

Both Candeias and Tavernier worked exceptionally well in tandem down the right-hand side of the pitch. Tavernier, in particular, showed the flexibility and tactical capability to make underlapping and overlapping runs depending on how each attack developed.

FIGURE 29

leg of the Europa League first qualifying round. Tavernier counter-pressed the defence well after a turnover, and the ball found its way to Candeias on the overlap. The Portuguese swung in an inviting cross which the keeper got to ahead of the on-rushing Alfredo Morelos. This showcased Tavernier's ability to drive infield into the right half-space, thus opening up several attacking opportunities for the team to try and take advantage of.

In the 22nd minute of the same game, Tavernier would provide the assist for the first goal of the Gerrard era. He again picked the ball up and made one of those now trademark runs into the right half-space; Candeias ran on the overlap, ready to receive the ball to swing into the box, as per the previous example. Instead on this occasion, Tavernier elected to switch the attack and play a pass across to the left-hand side of the box for Jamie Murphy, who had stayed wide to find himself a yard of space to carry the ball into the box and score the first goal of the Gerrard era.

A classic Tavernier assist came in the Europa League second qualifying round first leg against NK Osijek and is much more what could be classed as standard full-back play. The ball found its way to Tavernier following a corner on the right-hand side of the attack, not far from the edge of the opposition box. This angle at the edge of the box is one Tavernier favoured time and time again, as it allows him to deliver a first-time whipped cross into that corridor of uncertainty between the defence and the goalkeeper. On this occasion it would be Alfredo Morelos who connected with the ball to head Rangers into the lead in the 17th minute.

Croatian international Borna Barišić joined Rangers as a modern attacking full-back in the same mould as Tavernier, and fans were rightly excited at the thought of both players playing together and bringing balance to the flanks at Ibrox. Unfortunately, Barišić's first campaign at Rangers was less than stellar as he was impacted by two niggly injuries that kept him on the sidelines for three months. He earned a possibly unfair reputation of being a little too lightweight physically for the Scottish league in his debut season. He did show snippets of the player who played so well against Rangers for Osijek, but unfortunately, they were all too rare in that first campaign.

With Barišić unavailable, it was left to Jon Flanagan and Andy Halliday to fill in at left-back in 2018/19. Neither are natural left-backs, which is not uncommon even at the highest level of the game, but more importantly, it was felt that neither could provide the type of consistent creative output required of this role if Rangers were to become more flexible and have the capability to attack down both flanks.

Barišić started 2019/20 in the last-chance saloon as far as a sizeable majority of fans were concerned. Undoubtedly talented, there were concerns over his mentality to bounce back from a difficult first season. It's widely acknowledged that Barišić's entrance as a Rangers player came with his superb free kick against St Mirren in September of that second season. As good as that goal was, that was slightly premature as another injury in the very next game against Legia Warsaw in the Europa League play-off round – where he had looked timid and unsure in possession throughout – resulted in Barišić missing the subsequent 2-0 loss to Celtic at Ibrox.

Rangers went into this game in good form and high on confidence, but as mentioned earlier, Celtic would win the tactical battle and take the victory while putting a very early dent in Rangers' fledgling title ambitions. The Celtic game plan arguably surprised Rangers, but tellingly also showed them a significant amount of respect. Eyebrows were raised from the off as Celtic striker Odsonne Édouard kicked the ball out of play for a throw-in deep down Rangers' left straight from the kick-off. From this, Celtic pressed aggressively to limit Flanagan's options, resulting in the poor choice of a high throw to Jermain Defoe, which Scott Brown duly cut out. The marker had been set. Celtic's strategy in this game was focused on forcing Rangers to build play down their left and cutting off the passing lanes through aggressive and intelligent pressing.

Figure 30

Celtic's pressing strategy centred on taking advantage of Barišić's injury and targeting the left-hand side of the Rangers defence in two different ways. They cut off passing angles in a way that left Rangers with no option but to attempt to build play down their left-hand side with left-back Flanagan and left-sided centre-back Niko Katić, both right-footed and arguably the two least technical players in the team. Secondly, should both players receive the ball with an opponent near to them, they would be pressed intently to try and force a turnover of possession.

Flanagan in particular struggled to give Rangers any attacking intent in the left-back position. There were infrequent occasions that Steven Davis could release him in space down the left-hand side. In this example Flanagan receives one such pass, a sumptuous ball played over the Celtic defence but the Englishman would elect to delay the cross, cut back on to his favoured right foot and attempt to float a ball into the box – which was easily telegraphed and blocked by Celtic – rather than attempt to hit the byline and cut the ball back across the face of goal.

It would undeniably be the arrival of Barišić as an attacking force later in September 2019 that would bring a huge benefit to the team. As a natural left-footer with laser precision crossing ability, Barišić provided Rangers with the balance on either flank they craved, which they went on to utilise to maximum effect in the years following. An example of how significant an impact this had on the team manifested itself in January 2020, when both Barišić and Tavernier suffered minor injuries and spent a short spell on the sidelines. The impact to the team was keenly felt, just as it was a few months previous in that Celtic game. Flanagan, American utility man Matt Polster and Andy

FLANAGAN IN POSSESSION

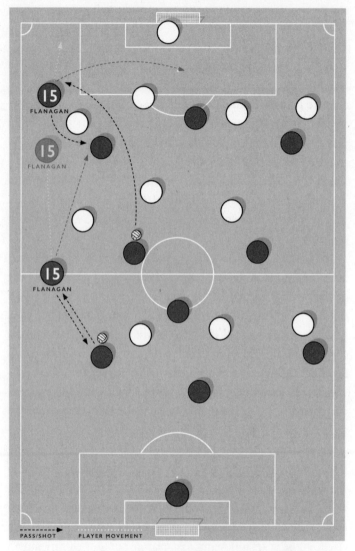

As a right-footed left-back, Flanagan's over-reliance on his stronger foot caused Rangers significant problems when trying to build attacks on the left flank.

FIGURE 30

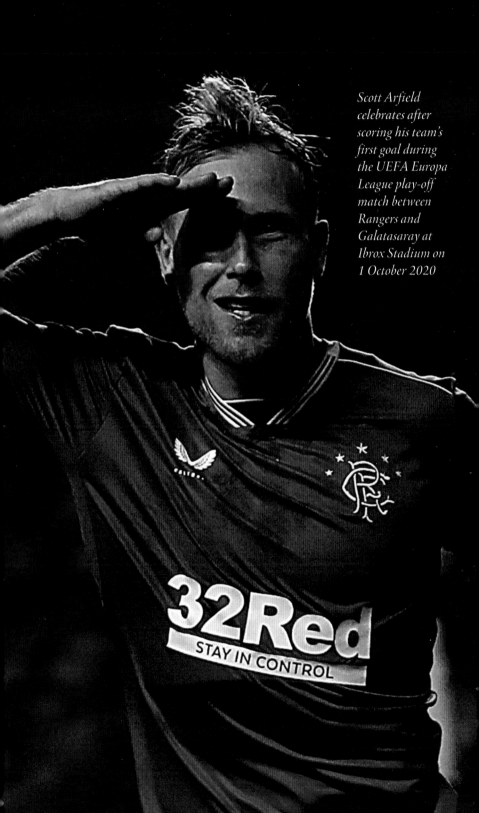

Scott Arfield celebrates after scoring his team's first goal during the UEFA Europa League play-off match between Rangers and Galatasaray at Ibrox Stadium on 1 October 2020

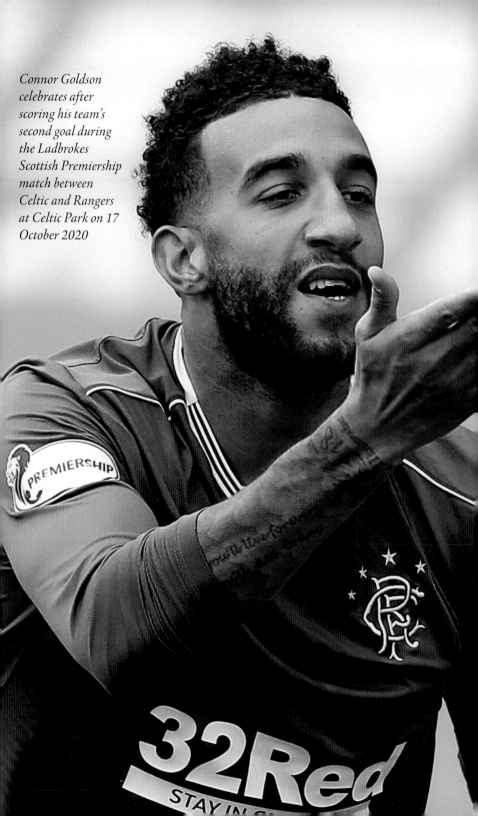

Connor Goldson celebrates after scoring his team's second goal during the Ladbrokes Scottish Premiership match between Celtic and Rangers at Celtic Park on 17 October 2020

Rangers' James Tavernier celebrates scoring his side's first goal of the game during the Scottish Premiership match at Tannadice Park, Dundee

Ianis Hagi celebrates scoring his side's third goal of the game during the UEFA Europa League round of 32 first leg match at Ibrox Stadium, Glasgow

Kemar Roofe celebrates after scoring his team's second goal during the UEFA Europa League Group D stage match between Standard Liege and Rangers at Stade Maurice Dufrasne on 22 October 2020

Alfredo Morelos of Rangers celebrates scoring the opening goal during the UEFA Europa League group G match against FC Porto at Ibrox Stadium

Steven Davis scores his team's first goal during the Scottish Cup game between Rangers and Celtic at Ibrox Stadium on 18 April 2021

Rangers' Ryan Kent celebrates his goal during the Ladbrokes Premiership match against Celtic at Celtic Park on 29 December 2019

James Tavernier of Rangers lifts the Scottish Premiership trophy after the match between Rangers and Aberdeen on 15 May 2021

Rangers coach Michael Beale gives instructions during a Scottish Premiership match between Rangers and St Mirren at Ibrox Stadium, on 6 March 2021

Rangers manager Steven Gerrard kisses the trophy as he celebrates winning the Scottish Premiership at Ibrox Stadium, Glasgow. Picture date: Saturday, 15 May 2021

Rangers' James Tavernier with the trophy after winning the Scottish Premiership at Ibrox Stadium

Halliday tried valiantly to deputise. Still, there was a massive chasm in Rangers' ability to dominate games and create high-quality goalscoring opportunities when deprived of their two most critical creative outlets. Nathan Patterson made his debut around this time in a Scottish Cup tie against Stranraer, but at just 18 years old, he was deemed not ready for the demands of regular first-team football and wasn't used again that season.

Barišić didn't look back from his emergence as a regular in the opening Europa League group stage game against Feyenoord in September 2019. He and Tavernier were the outstanding creative forces in the Scottish game for the next two seasons. Indeed, over the three-year period, the pair were responsible for an incredible total of 113 goals (49 goals, 64 assists) from full-back, which shows how integral they were to Rangers' tactical set-up. One could argue the system was built with maximising their potential in mind.

It's important to note that while both full-backs can be seen as similar as they were both offensive-minded the way Rangers utilised each from a tactical perspective was distinctly different. Barišić was more of a 'traditional' full-back if such a term still exists. He was not a player who was hugely involved in building attacks from deep, partly due to how one-footed he is. While Barišić would not usually elect to take his man on one vs one, he was very effective when combining with his near-side team-mates to progress the ball up the pitch. Ordinarily, Ryan Kent would look to pick up the ball in the left half-space and attempt to commit the right-back thus allowing Barišić to overload the flank. Glen Kamara was the team's insurance policy, either receiving the ball back, if space did not materialise or as the covering player should Barišić lose possession and be caught upfield.

Once Barišić received possession in the final third, he came alive. He was an elite crosser, capable of pinpoint deliveries on an incredibly consistent and regular basis. He would mostly receive the ball wide on the left and elect to whip in a curling delivery to the heart of the opposition penalty area, where it can cause maximum damage.

Figure 31

At times in the early years, Barišić's crossing could become a little one-dimensional, and when faced with tall, physical centre-backs, they were cleared with ease and the repetition of this meant they could lose their impact. As he grew into his role within the team, Barišić introduced some excellent cross variation to his play on the left, which yielded significant results. Throughout the three years, Barišić developed an almost telepathic relationship with Kamara and Kent on the left. While crossing is Barišić's key strength, how the team used this also varied depending on the scenario. All three of these players worked well in tandem when looking to manipulate space in the final third, particularly focusing on creating overloads to release Barišić in an advanced area to deliver a ball into the box.

In the first example on the left, we saw a traditional 'give and go' with Barišić passing the ball to Ryan Kent and running inside the full-back and centre-back in anticipation of receiving a one-two which he can then cut back into the box.

In example two, Barišić takes up a more traditional full-back crossing angle as he received a pass in a deeper area of the pitch than would usually be classed as his optimal area to deliver a ball into the box. In this instance, Barišić can either swing a high cross into the box to be attacked or – as he did during Rangers 1-1 away draw with Porto in the Europa League group stages – deliver an inch-perfect first-time pass to Morelos, who didn't need to break stride or take a touch before applying the finish.

Finally, Barišić was more than capable of getting beyond the full-backs on the outside and gambling on the midfielders' ability to play line-breaking passes between full-back and centre-back to cut defences open.

BARIŠIĆ

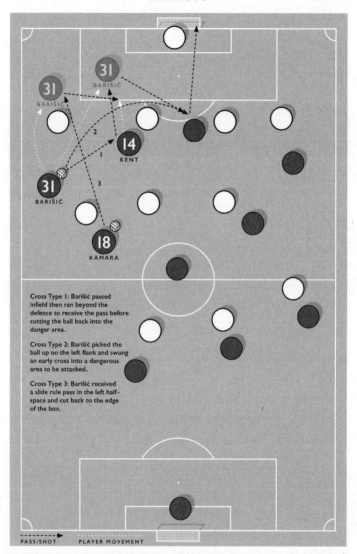

Cross Type 1: Barišić passed infield then ran beyond the defence to receive the pass before cutting the ball back into the danger area.

Cross Type 2: Barišić picked the ball up on the left flank and swung an early cross into a dangerous area to be attacked.

Cross Type 3: Barišić received a slide rule pass in the left half-space and cut back to the edge of the box.

PASS/SHOT — PLAYER MOVEMENT

As he grew into his role within the team, Barišić introduced some excellent cross variation to his play on the left, which yielded significant results.

FIGURE 31

Barišić is a prime example of how a player with a specific skillset can provide a completely different dimension to a team. Tavernier remained as the club's primary right-back but instead underwent a tactical evolution of his own during these three years. Tavernier's role developed into arguably that of an attacking number eight at various points within 2020/21 – again showing how flexible Gerrard's 4-3-3 system could be. Tavernier was always capable of driving infield when he has the ball, but in 2020/21 he took this to the next level, frequently ghosting in at the back post as a second striker for Barišić to find.

Figure 32

Tavernier's goal and Rangers' second against Galatasaray in the 2020/21 Europa League play-off round illustrated how important both full-backs were to the team, with Barišić providing the assist. This goal was much more than just that combination though and was really all about Tavernier's attacking dynamism given he started and finished the move. With that new freedom to arrive in the box with precision timing, he was able to provide another attacking threat, something Rangers had badly missed in the seasons previous.

Throughout 2020/21, Rangers continued to show flexibility and tweaked their full-backs from game to game – and sometimes in-game depending on the situation. Usually, Tavernier would be deployed higher than Barišić in an attempt to replicate the midfield set-up with Arfield or Aribo playing slightly more advanced than Glen Kamara but still offering maximum protection to the defence. Still, it was also not uncommon to see both full-backs sitting deeper in an attempt to draw an opponent out of their defensive shape and leave space in behind for the forwards to exploit.

Twice within a month, we would see this strategy employed slightly differently, but both garnered significant success. The most striking use was in the 5-1 victory against Motherwell

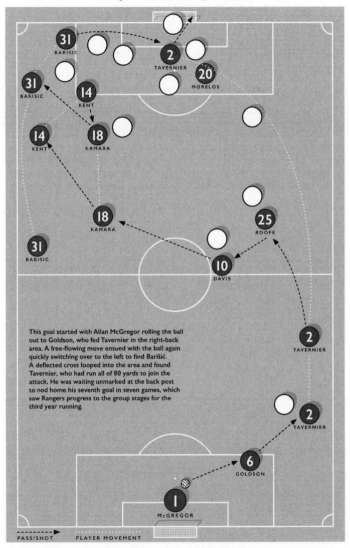

TAVERNIER ATTACKING THE BOX

Rangers 2-1 Galatasaray 01.10.20

This goal started with Allan McGregor rolling the ball
out to Goldson, who fed Tavernier in the right-back
area. A free-flowing move ensued with the ball again
quickly switching over to the left to find Barišić.
A deflected cross looped into the area and found
Tavernier, who had run all of 80 yards to join the
attack. He was waiting unmarked at the back post
to nod home his seventh goal in seven games, which
saw Rangers progress to the group stages for the
third year running.

PASS/SHOT   PLAYER MOVEMENT

This goal showcases how tactically astute the Rangers captain was. At times he would occupy the same
spaces as a number eight when Rangers attacked.

FIGURE 32

at Fir Park in late September, with Motherwell lining up in a 3-5-2 formation.

Figure 33

The positioning of Barišić is the most startling here, as his average position shows him almost level with Filip Helander, effectively performing in a back three in possession. That being said, it would be on the right where Rangers used the deeper full-back positioning to the most significant effect in this game. Rangers effectively played a game of cat and mouse with Motherwell, attempting to lure out right-back Stephen O'Donnell and Liam Grimshaw, filling in at left-back but generally more comfortable on the right. By asking both full-backs to sit deeper, Rangers lured Motherwell forward to press the ball, which left gaps in their defensive structure. The inclusion of Jordan Jones as a right-winger was met with surprise pre-game; however, his pace in behind was crucial, as evidenced by his excellent finish to put Rangers into a two-goal lead. With Grimshaw pressing Tavernier on the ball aggressively in his half, Rangers could overload down the right using Tavernier, Scott Arfield and Morelos to attack the space. A clever through ball by Arfield released Jones, who found himself in a foot race with left centre-back Rickie Lamie, who had been dragged out wide to cover. As expected, Jones beat his man with ease, cut inside and finished with aplomb in the bottom left-hand corner.

In the 2-0 win against Celtic at Parkhead a few weeks later, they too started in a 3-5-2 formation. Again both Rangers full-backs would position themselves slightly deeper at times and look to lure out Celtic's full-backs Diego Laxalt and Jeremie Frimpong before looking to drop balls into the channel for the pace of Brandon Barker and Ryan Kent to attack. In one situation during the first half, this approach resulted in Ryan Kent isolating Kristoffer Ajer in a wide position, forcing the Norwegian to foul him thus giving Rangers a free kick from

WITHDRAWN FULL-BACKS

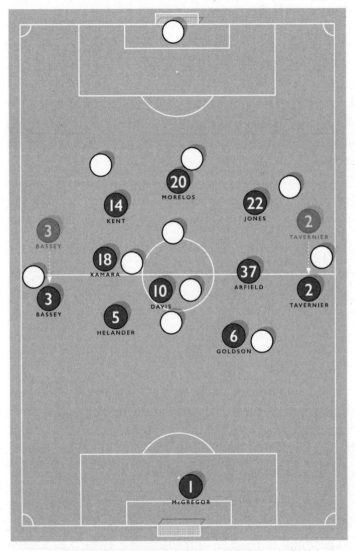

At points during the title winning season, Rangers would look to deploy their full-backs 10–15 yards deeper than usual as a deliberate tactic to draw an opposition out.

FIGURE 33

which they duly scored the opening goal. Flexibility was very much a key theme throughout this season.

Regardless, both players' styles remained unchanged even if their positions on the pitch did not, with Tavernier much more involved inside the pitch during build-up play yet still retaining that ability to whip inch-perfect crosses into the box from a slightly deeper angle. Barišić was still predominantly used as an overlapping full-back capable of delivering balls into the box from anywhere, but usually from a high and wide position on the left flank.

Throughout the season, both players played vital roles in ensuring Rangers only conceded those 13 league goals and continued to contribute outstanding numbers in the attacking third with that combined goal contribution of 46 in all competitions.

The emergence of 19-year-old Nathan Patterson in the latter half of the title-winning season gave Rangers another potentially outstanding full-back. Injuries to Tavernier and occasional stand-in right-back Leon Balogun in the Europa League round of 32 second leg against Royal Antwerp provided Patterson with an opportunity to show what he could offer to the team immediately, rather than as a prospect for the future. Replacing Balogun at half-time in the second leg, Patterson immediately had a positive impact. He latched on to a threaded through ball from Morelos in the 46th minute to beat the offside trap, drive into the box and smash home a right-footed shot to put Rangers 2-1 ahead on the night.

Given how similar his playing style is to Tavernier's, it's clear Patterson had put his short time with the first-team squad to good use so far. The only discernible stylistic difference was Patterson's preference to dribble and take on his defender one vs one. In contrast, Tavernier preferred to build attacks through combination play with midfielders and forwards. This is another example of ways Rangers retain a significant degree of flexibility within their heavily structured tactical set-up simply by selecting a different player in the starting 11. Despite Tavernier having his best campaign to date in a Rangers jersey and still being in his peak as a footballer, there will always be opportunities to rotate whether unforced or forced through injury as was the case here. The biggest compliment to Patterson during this period was that the team did not look any weaker with him in it.

The Number Six

'We've changed slightly the way we are playing, not a lot, probably the movement of five or ten yards with the two wide attackers, full-backs being a bit more adventurous. We're really trying to emphasise the midfielders getting on the ball and playing together, and I think that has been a really welcome addition to the team. Not playing with a traditional battling, holding midfielder and going more with a footballer in Steven Davis and I think he's really jumped to that challenge as well.'

Michael Beale, The Scotsman, *April 2019*

The initial transformation on the pitch was immediate over that first summer with Gerrard in charge, but from the January 2019 transfer window onwards it was clear that gradual evolution was a key focus of the entire club.

This was evident both on and off the pitch throughout his tenure, from sports science to the embedding of a modern, flexible tactical approach under the watchful eye of Michael Beale, to the sharp upturn in quality – and most importantly suitability – of the first-team squad. No stone was left unturned, and every marginal gain was analysed, deconstructed, and put back together again in the ongoing quest for glory. One could argue with a fair degree of certainty that throughout this time, the most challenging – and therefore potentially the most satisfying – on-pitch transformation materialised in the centre of midfield. As a famed midfielder himself, it was only natural that Gerrard put a key focus on this area of the team from the off.

The central midfielders who featured most frequently in the early months under Gerrard were Ryan Jack, Ross McCrorie and three of the summer signings – Lassana Coulibaly, who joined on loan from Ligue 1 Angers, Liverpool loanee Ovie Ejaria and Canadian international Scott Arfield. The team was set up in that basic 4-3-3 formation outlined in the 2018/19 Season Overview section and in these embryonic times, the roles and duties for the midfield three were pretty conventional and functional, none more so than the lone defensive midfielder, or single pivot as it has come to be known.

Ross McCrorie, the former captain of the under-20 team, had progressed through the ranks, making his debut in the season previous to replace Bruno Alves in a League Cup tie against Partick Thistle. Then manager Pedro Caixinha described McCrorie as 'the future of this country, not only this club, as a centre-half'. High praise indeed for a 19-year-old making his debut. Unfortunately, the Caixinha regime fizzled out shortly after, and under caretaker manager Graeme Murty, McCrorie enjoyed a mixed spell playing as either a defensive midfielder or at centre-back. A couple of heavy defeats to Celtic in quick succession did his central defensive prospects significant damage at the end of the season, but he was still considered a key prospect for the future and certainly a player who it was hoped would play his part in the squad as the new era dawned. During those dark pre-Gerrard times, there was a tendency to try to search for any glimmer of hope admist the gloom and as a Rangers fan and youth academy prospect McCrorie would come to symbolise that.

'We had a player playing at centre-back position when wasn't his real position, who was 19 years of age and thrown in at the deep end, who could have been destroyed in terms of his career,' Gerrard told the *Scottish Sun* just one day after his team's first competitive game, against FK Shkupi. It was clear to see that he didn't see McCrorie playing long-term at Rangers as a centre-back, despite the proclamations of previous managers.

McCrorie started Gerrard's first two games playing alongside Ryan Jack in a 4-2-3-1 formation. Coulibaly offered a similar physical profile to McCrorie and was also used in this role at times, so it was clear that the coaching staff had identified their skillsets as key to their tactical approach in the early weeks. McCrorie, however, quickly found his appearances in the team limited as the weeks progressed, with the manager favouring players with more ability on the ball when Rangers had possession in the attacking phase.

The number six in Gerrard's team was expected to contribute fully in both the defensive and the offensive phases of play. In the early months, the player situated in this role at the base of the midfield would be classed as more of a traditional destroyer when Rangers did not have possession, using his physique and mobility to harry opposition midfielders, win the ball back and recycle play. This player would also be responsible for providing defensive cover for both full-backs. Therefore, playing as a single defensive midfielder, he would be required to shift laterally across the defensive midfield area depending on any pockets of space that may present themselves for opposition attackers to exploit.

The single holding midfielder also needed to provide a solid base for the team's attacking play. As most teams will not solely build attacks using their centre-backs' passing range, it is vital to have a deep-lying midfielder who is proficient in possession and can position himself intelligently to receive and make passes quickly. This ensures clean build-up play through the lines against teams who sit deep in a defensive block. This is especially important when you consider that Rangers pushed their full-backs aggressively high and wide when in possession, meaning the number six was often the only option available to receive a pass. In these scenarios, having a player in this role who was press-resistant, could receive the ball under pressure and pass through the lines could be considered more advantageous than a traditional defensive midfielder.

Figure 34

When selected in the team, Coulibaly and Arfield would act as a pair of aggressive, hard-running box-to-box midfielders tasked with attempting to control the midfield and progressing the ball into the attacking third of the pitch. Coulibaly played his part in this team in that first season; however, as with McCrorie, there was a strong argument that he did most of his good work out of possession. Most assumed that he wasn't at the technical level required in the creative sense to become a first-pick Rangers midfielder.

As Ovie Ejaria found out, though, having essentially the opposite skillset wasn't quite enough either. Rangers utilised the Liverpool connection to bring in Ejaria on loan, and he repaid that faith with the goal that sent the team into the Europa League group stages. This was a monumental achievement given that the squad had been thrown together in a very brief pre-season and had to negotiate four qualifying rounds so early in the season. Ejaria's ability on the ball in midfield was certainly something that could be beneficial to Rangers, as having a player in there who was more than capable of picking a pass and carrying the ball forward in attack was desirable. Still, as you would expect from a young loanee, the midfielder possibly lacked the consistent quality to impact games in Scotland every week. This wouldn't be the first time Rangers would look to use a player with this type of skillset, another indication of the coaching staff's desire to mould the team into their style over a period of time. Despite playing regularly, Ejaria's impact was limited before he elected to cut his loan short and return to Liverpool in early January 2019.

MIDFIELD DESTROYER

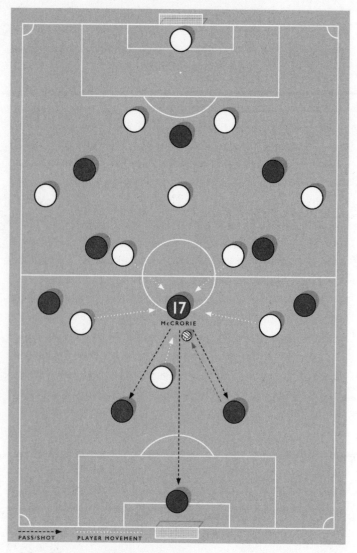

In Gerrard's first season, the deepest-lying central midfielder could be classed as more of a destroyer than a ball-playing number six which caused issues during attacking build-up.

FIGURE 34

That same month, Rangers moved to heavily reinforce their central midfield options by recruiting former captain Steven Davis as he re-joined initially on a six-month loan from Southampton. Ex-Arsenal midfielder Glen Kamara also signed on a pre-contract from Dundee, a deal which was made permanent a few weeks later in the window for the princely sum of £50,000. Despite the stuttering start to the calendar year and a league title challenge that quickly fizzled out, the return of Davis provided a calming influence in the number six role and while he took his time to readjust to the physical demands of the league, his quality was never in doubt. His signing necessitated that slight change in style, too; gone were the battling qualities of a McCrorie or Coulibaly at the base of midfield, and in their stead was a specialist deep-lying playmaker.

Irrespective of his excellent technical ability, Davis's positional awareness and reading of the game was a key factor of his role when out of possession and allowed Rangers to use his passing skills in that defensive midfield role. He was not tasked with regularly breaking from his deep starting position and pressing the opposition into losing the ball. Instead, he played to his strengths and remained vital in anticipating danger nearer to Rangers' goal either intercepting a pass or tackling the attacking player to regain possession.

The thought process was clear, as were the tangible benefits of the move from a destroyer to a playmaker. Despite Davis advancing into his twilight years as a player, he was still an accomplished midfielder who now played in a deeper position on the pitch than Rangers fans would have been used to seeing him in from his previous stint. During his first spell under Walter Smith at the turn of the last decade, Davis was utilised in a more energetic role on the right of the midfield – similar in style to the role Claudio Reyna played at the club during the late 1990s. At the grand old age of 34, though, his pace had started to erode; therefore, a deeper role was gradually introduced during his time at Southampton.

The player who returned took a while to get up to speed with playing regular football again following a stop-start 18 months prior, but Davis would go on to perform that classic number six role in such a crucial, composed way.

Rangers had neatly evolved from utilising a holding midfielder or destroyer playing at the base of midfield to a player who wanted to be proficient in taking the ball from centre-backs and building attacks from deep, a small but significant change. Irrespective of that, Davis provided a much higher level of ability in this position, which was of sizeable benefit to the team.

Davis had the vision and technique to receive the ball, scan the pitch, and play the pass in one fluid movement, which opened up so many more options to Rangers when progressing the ball forward. With such abilities both on and off the ball, Davis effectively became press-resistant, meaning opposition attackers would very rarely be able to force him into losing possession as he was too quick of feet and of thought to allow this to happen. As a centre-back, having a player who can receive the ball in any manner of situations and on either foot provides a considerable level of comfort, and Davis was one of the best at doing just that.

An under-rated aspect of Davis's job as the deep-lying playmaker was his ability to pick a pass into the attacking areas of the pitch. His role in build-up play should not be understated as while he was not exactly famed as a proficient dribbler capable of beating two men, he could take defenders out of the game with a quick shift of the hips and cute pass through the lines to the attackers.

Figure 35

There were also times when Rangers elected to play with two defensive midfielders forming a double pivot in front of the defence. More often than not, Kamara would drop slightly deeper next to Davis and act as an energetic foil. Davis would

DESTROYER TO PLAYMAKER

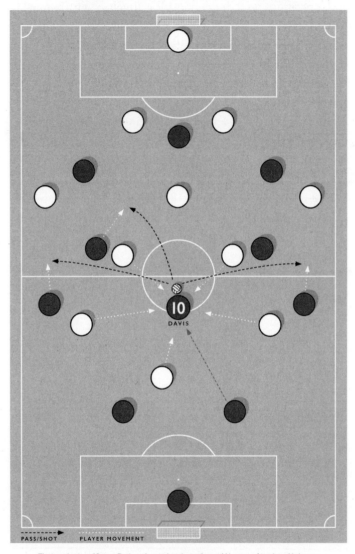

PASS/SHOT   PLAYER MOVEMENT

The introduction of Steven Davis as the number six was key and his range of passing added a new dimension to Rangers' play.

FIGURE 35

play on the right-hand side in these instances, take up slightly wider positions, and drag opposition attackers with him while Rangers were in possession. This would, in turn, open up passing lanes to allow centre-backs such as Goldson to either stride forward and build play himself, or pass directly into the central areas of the pitch, thus creating different layers to Rangers' attacks.

Beloved by the vast majority of Rangers supporters for his understated personality and style, no one could conceivably say that Davis was underrated as a player given fans fully appreciated that his role in the team was one of the most crucial. This was evidenced by the tactical flexibility he displayed, his calmness under pressure and his ability to more than match any physical battle that came his way in either domestic or continental football.

Flat Midfield Three

'As a midfielder, I was jealous of Ryan Jack's performance tonight. It was stunning. I had watched Ryan from the outside before I came here and I knew about his big move from Aberdeen. But it's not until you get close up to these players that you see what they are about and how hungry they are, how they live their lives. I think I have got a good type on my hands there. He is a player who cares, who wants to win and is prepared to go out on the pitch and do exactly what you have asked of him.'

Steven Gerrard on Jack in The Scotsman

If that shift from destroyer to playmaker could be classed as the first evolution of Gerrard's Rangers midfield, then the second has to be the introduction of what came to be known as the 'flat midfield three'. This development of Gerrard's midfield would come just a few months later and was introduced almost as a by-product of the arrivals of Davis and Kamara a few months prior. The subsequent result and impact on the centre of the pitch was as far from the image of the swashbuckling ex-Liverpool central midfielder's playing style as you could imagine.

As the team's fortunes stuttered in the early part of 2019, a 2-1 defeat to their Old Firm rivals in late March left morale at a fairly low ebb with the title tilt all but lost with seven games remaining. The progress throughout the season had been undeniable, but the team knew they would finish the season empty-handed domestically, which has never been deemed acceptable at Rangers. Under Gerrard, they were a team capable on their day of being a match for most opponents at home and abroad, as evidenced by victories over Celtic and some notable positive results in the Europa League qualification and group stages. Throughout that season, the team had struggled to exert control on certain matches, and there was still an undeniable counter-attacking feel to the general approach at times. At home, most teams would sit in and encourage Rangers to try and break them down, but in away games or against higher quality opposition, Rangers could better utilise their strength on the break. On the flip side, with a midfield not adept at asserting themselves thoroughly on the game to suffocate an opposition, Rangers were still vulnerable on the counter-attack themselves, particularly given how aggressive Gerrard now wanted his full-backs to be in possession.

With the league dream over for another season and eluding Rangers for the first time under Gerrard, there was an opportunity to experiment in the remaining games with eyes on the next season. In the very next fixture following that Celtic defeat – a 3-0 victory at Ibrox against Hearts in early April – Rangers debuted a new 4-3-2-1 formation which included Davis, Kamara and Ryan Jack lining up for the first time as a trio.

We refer to this system as a flat midfield three, but it's a loose definition in reality. All three players have similar tendencies to that of a number six or a deep-lying playmaker, but Davis would be the deepest player more often than not and would assume this specific role throughout the three seasons.

This relatively meaningless end-of-season game would be rather crucial in the overall tactical evolution of this team as also debuting for the first time, was Rangers' 'twin tens'. Kent and Arfield were asked to play ten yards narrower to give more support to Jermain Defoe, enjoying a run in the team due to another suspension for Alfredo Morelos.

Around this time, comparisons would start to be drawn more regularly with Liverpool's tactical set-up under Jürgen Klopp. This flat, compact three was very reminiscent of the Liverpool midfield trio, a functional and robust base on which their myriad of attacking talent could prosper. But it was much more than that, and over the next 12 months, it became the core of the Rangers team.

Kamara played as the left-sided central midfielder nominally, but the Finnish international was really capable of playing anywhere in midfield and adapting seamlessly to any situation or tactical role. In the early seasons under Gerrard, Kamara was deployed as a number six and, therefore, the deepest-lying midfielder intermittently – usually in the absence of Davis rather than as a pair. On more than one occasion, his defensive awareness and decision-making when picking passes in those key areas left a lot to be desired and his time spent in this deeper position reduced as the months slipped by.

Kamara's skillset was not hugely different to that of Davis, although his creative passing could be improved if this was required for his tactical role. Where Kamara excelled was in providing the platform for the rest of the team to attack. He was the tactical chameleon of the group; with such a wide and varied skillset, Kamara was theoretically capable of playing in at least seven of Rangers' ten outfield positions. He acted as the glue that bound the left side of Rangers' tactical structure together alongside Borna Barišić and Ryan Kent. Should Barišić lose possession and be caught upfield, Kamara was the one to shuttle wide and look to prevent counter-attacks. If an opposition team decided to overload Rangers' left flank, there he was to provide support to his man and regain possession of the ball.

These were vital skills in this tactical set-up and he was hugely influential, particularly in European games where the extra space and time on the ball gave him the platform to shine. Despite his skillset being focused more towards tactical discipline and ball retention, he did foray forwards once or twice to contribute to the attack. His most memorable goal came against Benfica in the Estádio da Luz in November 2020 during the Europa League group stage. He collected a clever switch of play from Alfredo Morelos following a counter-attack, shifted his weight on to his right foot and slotted the ball home from just outside the area to give Rangers a 2-1 lead on the night.

Ryan Jack arguably went through the most considerable evolution of the three throughout his first four years at the club. Signed from Aberdeen on a free transfer by then boss Pedro Caixinha, Jack's role had primarily been that of a classic defensive midfielder tasked with receiving the ball from the defence and looking to build attacks. Jack's combative nature did not go down well with Scottish referees now that he played for the country's biggest club. Jack was sent off in four of his first 22 appearances for Rangers, which resulted in the midfielder speaking to a sports psychologist to get to the root of the problem. A slight tweak was needed to his playing style in that first season to avoid spending (more) months sitting in the stand. The theory among Rangers fans that bigger teams in Scotland are refereed differently was certainly tested given that Jack had never previously been classed as that kind of player throughout his years in Aberdeen. As that 2017/18 season fell apart and Gerrard was announced as the new manager, it was felt that this would be a massive opportunity for Jack to work under both Gerrard and famed ex-Scottish international midfielder Gary McAllister.

Jack was deployed in both number six and number eight positions within the Rangers midfield and performed effectively in that first season, despite the team's well-documented travails. Gerrard had been fulsome in his praise of the midfielder since day one, even going as far as to say he 'was jealous' of Jack's performance, following a particularly impressive showing in just his fourth competitive game under the new manager, in the 1-1 draw with NK Osijek which saw Rangers advance into the Europa League third qualifying round.

High praise indeed, and words which would ultimately be validated by the vital role Jack would go on to play in the team throughout the manager's tenure. In Gerrard's second season, at times Jack was given much more licence to roam forward, almost as a precursor to the 'free eight' central midfield roles we would see introduced the following season. He was capable of playing this role to sometimes great effect, particularly in a virtuoso all-action display away to Ross County in October 2019 where his driving runs from deep culminated in him scoring two outstanding goals from outside the box.

But as a player who appeared more comfortable building play from deep and connecting the team together rather than playing ahead of the ball or with his back to goal, it was not something that appeared to be a long-term solution if Rangers wanted to add attacking thrust and creativity into the middle of the park. Still, Jack showed fantastic flexibility to adapt to the tweaks the coaching staff introduced and the improvement in his passing range throughout this period was apparent for all to see. His anticipation and positioning skills were always exemplary and similar to Kamara on the opposite side, he would always be available for a pass under pressure, provide cover or pick up the slack for a team-mate in trouble.

To describe the midfield trio of Jack, Davis and Kamara as solid or functional is to do the three a disservice. Each player has a built-in flexibility and skillset to play in several different roles within any midfield set-up, as shown throughout their time at Rangers and their previous careers. While they are all excellent in possession of the ball and on a positional and tactical level, it's not unfair to say all three were completely similar on a stylistic level.

Coming into 2019/20 and with the emergence of Barišić as a first pick and significant attacking threat on the left, Rangers now had two flying full-backs who the coaching staff had deliberately asked to play higher and more aggressively. With the flat midfield three dominating the centre of the midfield, Rangers had reduced but not eradicated the threat of being caught on the counter-attack.

The next tweak for the midfield would become apparent almost immediately. Rangers' late defensive capitulation to Young Boys in the Europa League group stage saw the team lose 2-1 to a 93rd-minute goal by Christian Fassnacht. While the team would still go on to qualify from their group and secure European football after Christmas for the first time in nine years, Rangers' lack of control in failing to see out a 1-1 draw was laid bare with a simple ball over the top when the game was stretched proving fatal. There would be no repeat in their next European game, a 1-1 draw away to Porto, with Rangers producing arguably their finest 90 minutes of the Gerrard era to that point. Porto had a pair of attacking full-backs themselves in the shape of Jesús Corona and Alex Telles, and there was a risk of an end-to-end game developing because of this. Still, the way Kamara and Jack shackled them was remarkable. In possession, the pair constantly provided out-balls into the midfield for the centre-backs and full-backs by rotating their positions effectively to free themselves from Porto's pressure. When out of possession and facing counter-attacks, they were on hand to double up with their full-back and snuff out danger or win control back effectively.

A key facet of this excellent result was a small but significant tweak to the central midfield set-up resulting in the two wider central midfielders, Kamara and Jack, being asked to cover space laterally rather than vertically. In short, this meant that when Borna Barišić attacked, Kamara's primary function was to shuffle over and ensure Rangers had the appropriate level of defensive cover. The same was true on the right side, with Jack tasked with dropping in during James Tavernier's frequent forays into the attack. Given Rangers' width and creativity came from the full-back areas, the team were naturally also susceptible to overloads; therefore, the tweak to support them provided significant additional benefits.

Figure 36

This now provided Rangers with a solid base in both defensive and offensive phases of play. Three central attackers supported by the two attacking full-backs ensured they were well set up as a cohesive team in both phases. This latest evolution was much improved on the season prior; indeed, many have said that this autumn period in 2019 could be classed as the high point of Rangers' tactical style, with the players regularly dominating high-quality opposition in a way that no Ibrox side in living memory had done. But part of what makes football so special is that no tactical approach or style is ever completely infallible and that was also the case here.

As is the case at Rangers, when the team is winning, everything is rosy in the garden. But should results turn – sometimes even just one result – then so can fan opinion very quickly. The flat midfield three was revered in significant victories against Celtic and in Europe but quickly became a source of frustration in domestic games where the three players would appear to position themselves in a straight line and offer a minimal attacking threat from the central areas to provide support when breaking down more defensive teams. Given the team's well-documented struggles in beating the low block in Gerrard's first two seasons, these criticisms appeared to have some foundation.

In Rangers' 1-0 victory against St Mirren at Ibrox in January 2020, Jack, Davis and Kamara all started in the midfield three as the home side dominated but lacked the attacking quality to win by a more comfortable margin. A pattern began to emerge whereby the more possession Rangers had, the less success they had in the game. Possession is desired, but sterile possession without any purpose is not optimal for a team like Rangers. The average positions from this game also show how

PORTO 1-1 RANGERS

Estádio do Dragão Europa League 24.10.19

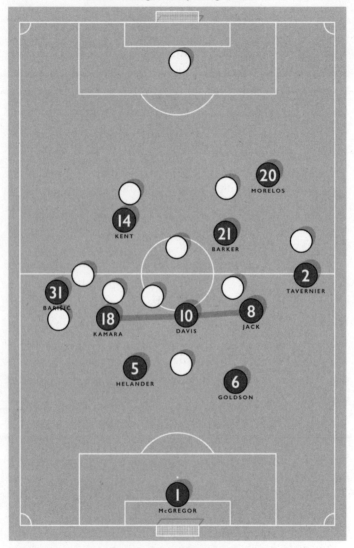

Rangers' 'narrow and compact defensive shape' was never more evident than in this game as the team constantly forced Porto into wider areas of the pitch.

FIGURE 36

similar the three players were, with each occupying the same horizontal lines of the pitch. The need for variance of skillset and player positioning was becoming more pressing with each passing week.

Figure 37

By offering a limited threat from midfield, it was easier for teams to funnel Rangers attacks into less dangerous wider areas and force the full-backs to play high balls into the box. Given Rangers' striking options were limited to Alfredo Morelos and Jermain Defoe, this threat was managed fairly convincingly on the whole by most opposing centre-backs. Rangers had managed to achieve stability and control in the middle of the park. Still, the team had suffocated themselves in possession at times and badly needed to adapt as Gerrard's second season drew parallels with the first as the team again struggled following the winter break and limped to that COVID-enforced close.

If season one under Gerrard could be neatly summed up by the switch from a destroyer-type central midfielder to a deep-lying playmaker, then the second was all about the robust and compact midfield three working together as a unit for the benefit of the whole team. The third and final evolution would come in the third season and would see Rangers reap significant attacking benefits from their revised midfield approach.

RANGERS 1 - 0 ST MIRREN

Ibrox Stadium SPFL 22.01.20

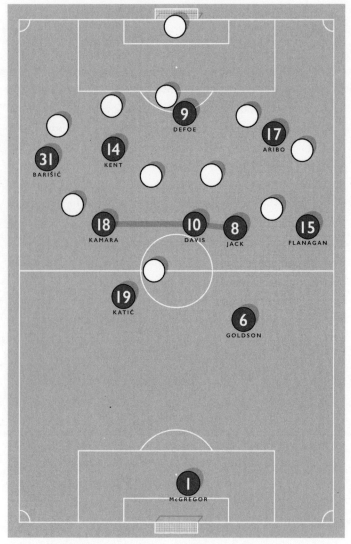

The 'flat midfield three' that had served Rangers well was fast becoming too rigid and devoid of attacking threat from the middle.

FIGURE 37

Free Eights

'We've gone with a midfielder less and put another one further forward because we're coming up against a block. Just to be a bit more bold and ambitious, to create more problems. But we've got the options on the bench to flip from a midfield three to a two. At the moment, the formation and the personnel have been working well.'

Steven Gerrard, The Athletic, *August 2020*

In the early stages of his third season at the helm, Gerrard pointedly mentioned on more than one occasion that a key aim for the campaign was for the team to become more 'bold and ambitious'. Speaking to The Athletic following a 3-0 league victory over St Johnstone in August 2020, Gerrard was asked whether he had found the right midfield balance already, in just the third league game of the season and the above quote was his answer.

In this game, Rangers had switched to a rarely used 4-2-3-1 formation, with the assumed intent to play with a more recognisable number ten in Joe Aribo positioned just behind Morelos as the lone striker. With Kamara and Jack sitting deeper in a double pivot providing a solid barrier, Rangers could provide commensurate defensive assurance yet also gain an additional attacker in the final third of the pitch. In three of their next four league games, Rangers would use this formation with the 0-0 draw away to Livingston being the only fixtures where they reverted back to 4-3-3 and sterile possession with minimal attacking thrust.

St Johnstone (3-0), Kilmarnock (2-0) and Dundee United (4-0) were all dispatched comfortably using the 4-2-3-1 formation; therefore, it was naturally assumed that Rangers had finally uncovered the key to breaking down low blocks consistently and would look to adopt this system from here on. However, this did not prove to be the case as Rangers switched back to their favoured 4-3-2-1 for the next match, an uncharacteristically chaotic 2-2 draw against Hibs. In this game, Scott Arfield would display great offensive prowess from a central midfield role peaking with an excellent goal, another well-rehearsed training ground move which showcased some key repetitions from Rangers' work on the training pitch.

It's fair to say that some specific formations, and the selection of players with a particular skillset, can work better in certain games or even scenarios within games than others. The key is to find a balance that complements the players at your disposal and the problem you are trying to solve in the shape of the opposition.

During his time as head coach of Liverpool's academy teams, Michael Beale spoke on several occasions about how vital creating a balanced and flexible midfield blend is to the tactical evolution of any team. At a seminar he delivered to Northern Irish coaches in Larne in 2016, he again spoke at length about this subject but went into forensic detail on the different roles that could comprise the midfield unit.

He used terms such as destroyer, energiser, spider, passer and magician to describe the tactical roles of a modern midfield three. Very different to the more traditional names regularly used when discussing players' roles such as number six, number eight and number ten.

Beale explained to *The Athletic*, 'It can be a two with a one in front, a one with a two in front, or it can be a flat three. It doesn't matter. What matters is that there are different personalities.

'He can be an energiser. That's classic [Jordan] Henderson at the minute – someone a bit old-fashioned, who works the channels and is very energetic, up and down.

'He can be a passer. Gerrard went from an energiser to a passer at the end of his career. A magician would be like [Philippe] Coutinho, who likes to ride in between the lines like a David Silva, can receive it and twist and turn.

'When that magician is not creating and scoring, I think he becomes a spider in the web. He's like Xavi: if you take him out, you realise he's not there, but what we can be guilty of sometimes is, "Well, if you don't score many, you don't stop many, and you don't assist many" ... but he's the connector. He links everything together.

'Then, there is the old-fashioned destroyer, like Roy Keane. You want to have a blend. I have seen loads of coaches work on rotation in midfield. If you play someone who likes to go into the ball and is a passer, someone who likes running and someone who likes to ride in between the lines, you will get a lovely blend.

'It's more about personality. You can probably have two [similar] – and players do fit in between. There's no reason why you can't break the game up as a destroyer and be a good passer, there's no reason why you can't be a magician and a spider in the web but you try to not have three of the same one if you're trying to get a blend.'

It's a fascinating insight into the thought process of team building and how coaches attempt to create the perfect midfield blend to suit the players they currently have at their disposal and the challenges they may face game to game. The clear evolution throughout Gerrard and Beale's time at the club is clear to see when we begin to assign the midfield players to these tactical roles. In the early months of their first season, the midfield three primarily constituted a mix of destroyers and energisers. The destroyers were Scotland under-21 international and now Aberdeen player Ross McCrorie and Angers loanee Lassana Coulibaly, a dynamic and aggressive box-to-box midfielder.

As per Beale's descriptions, Ryan Jack and Scott Arfield were two who could fill several of these categories. At various stages of his career, Jack has arguably filled three of these roles – destroyer and passer at Aberdeen, evolving into the hybrid of a passer and energiser that we see now at Rangers. Arfield could be classed as filling several also, but certainly throughout 2018/19 would be tagged as an energiser primarily as both he and Jack used their power and tenacity to connect defence and attack from the right-hand side of midfield. With Glen Kamara (spider) and Steven Davis (passer) joining midway through that first season, Rangers were well stocked with an excellent complement of destroyers, energisers, passers and spiders in the web during Gerrard's first 18 months.

They needed some unpredictability, and as has been well documented they needed some consistent attacking quality from deeper central areas. Rangers' opponents knew that they had a reasonable chance of stopping Rangers if they stopped Tavernier, Kent and Morelos from getting on the ball in dangerous areas. They were quite content to come to Ibrox, sit deep and double mark those players to tempt Rangers into attempting to break them down. A sizeable chunk of the time, this strategy worked, too.

What the team craved was some magic and some end product.

When you hear the phrase number eight, what Rangers player do you see in your head? If you didn't conjure up an image of Paul Gascoigne rampaging through the middle of the pitch at Ibrox to score his and Rangers' second goal against Aberdeen in May 1996 to clinch eight in a row, then I'm sorry, but you're doing it wrong. Gazza was the archetypal 1990s number eight, a swashbuckling central midfielder capable of dominating games, creating goals for his team-mates and finishing chances himself. A number eight needs to have the capability to make those lung-busting, box-to-box runs to help out his defensive colleagues and also provide support to his forwards in attacking scenarios. Of course, taking away that Rangers player perspective, Steven Gerrard is arguably the outstanding number eight British football has produced in the last 25 years. Therefore, we watched with more than a bit of intrigue as he began to evolve the Rangers engine room even further.

During his time in the English Championship and Premier League with Burnley, Scott Arfield tended to play more as a wide midfielder in a disciplined 4-4-2 with the tactical instruction to tuck in and provide additional protection to the two central midfielders. At Rangers, it was clear from the off that he was to be given more creative licence to act as a conduit between midfield and attack with his dynamic style and strong off-ball running. Not the most noted or incisive passer, Rangers utilised his industrious technique and movement in a way that encouraged Arfield to get beyond the strikers and make an impact in the final third. He had that gloriously rare knack of finding himself in the right place at the right time in dangerous areas. Decision-making and efficiency can be erratic; however, he did finish Gerrard's debut season with 12 goals and six assists – a career-best to that point.

Arfield struggled with fitness and consistency issues throughout his first three seasons at the club, and even when playing, he could be classed as frustrating. He was the type of player who so often *nearly* scored a great goal or *almost* linked up with another player only for a tiny change in wavelength, causing a pass to go astray. These split-second decisions that go wrong can look harsher when watching the game live, but players like Arfield live and die by that risk as they know that the benefits can be massive when it comes off. Rather than stifling this side of Arfield's game, Rangers would look to recruit players on the same wavelength as him and who would be sharp enough to see his run or benefit from his combination play at the edge of the box.

Due to the prominence of the Davis, Kamara and Jack trio, Arfield had been repurposed as a right-sided number ten in the six months leading up to a match against Aberdeen in September 2019. In Rangers' 4-3-2-1 formation, his link-up play, goal threat and dynamism on that side of the pitch acted as a much-needed balance to Kent's explosive dribbling skills on the left.

In this match, Arfield was deployed back in central midfield alongside Jack and Davis, with Greg Stewart occupying the attacking slot on the right-hand side, and throughout the 90 minutes we saw how valuable Arfield could be playing in what we can now class as a 'free eight' position. This term was first heard in British football to describe Pep Guardiola's use of Kevin De Bruyne and David Silva during his first season at Manchester City in 2016.

Both City players began their careers as wingers who had started to drift into more central number ten areas as tactics evolved in the 2010s and wingers became part of a more fluid and flexible front three. Later, as the battle to control the centre of the pitch became all-encompassing, they would be pulled back even further. Despite the starting position being primarily in the central midfield, both players would play the role of a traditional number eight and number ten hybrid.

'It's a different role,' De Bruyne told the Belgian newspaper *Het Laatste Nieuws*. 'It's all right. It's a little change but it's all right. The coach has his own tactics. I play not as a number ten but as a free eight with a lot of movement everywhere.'

Guardiola is a master tactician, but his use of players in different areas of the pitch not traditionally associated with their skillset marks him out as a true innovator. His coaching career is littered with examples of breaking the norms to gain an advantage in every conceivable area of the pitch, from switching

Lionel Messi to a false nine at Barcelona, turning Philipp Lahm into a world-class central midfielder at Bayern Munich, or winning the Premier League at City with Fabian Delph as a converted left-back.

That day against Aberdeen, Arfield displayed everything Rangers lacked from the middle with his direct running and clever link-up play. He combined very well with Stewart – who played very well in what was a rare start. Arfield provided a cutting edge from central midfield that had been largely absent while still maintaining the same defensive work ethic previously employed by the trio of Davis, Jack and Kamara. Rangers' incisive passing game coupled with their rotational movement was a joy to watch, and it was the key to them finally solving the Aberdeen puzzle and tearing apart their ultra-defensive strategy.

Aberdeen, under Derek McInnes, adopted an aggressive man-marking approach when playing Rangers, so much so that it wasn't uncommon to see their right-back Shay Logan follow Ryan Kent all the way over the other side of the pitch like a puppy trailing its master. It undeniably worked, as Aberdeen and Kilmarnock – two dogged and disciplined defensive teams over this period – had terrific records against Rangers. While he didn't score or provide any assists, Arfield gave Aberdeen a torrid time throughout and his guile coupled with the movement and aggression of Stewart, Kent and Morelos. Having players move with such regularity off the ball caused chasms to appear in the Aberdeen defence which created opening after opening and allowed Rangers to take advantage to full effect as they ran out very comfortable 5-0 winners.

Before this game, Gerrard had only managed to defeat Aberdeen twice in seven attempts, 4-2 at Pittodrie and 2-0 in one of the final games of the season prior. Asking Arfield to attack through the lines and also crucially engaging in that positional rotation with Stewart – who was a similar type of player but playing in a different area of the pitch – resulted in

Aberdeen being unable to mark as diligently or successfully as they had done in those earlier matches. Combined with Morelos dropping deep and Tavernier driving forward on the underlap, these rotations created chaos in the Aberdeen defence, with four of the five goals coming from the right side of the pitch.

Figure 38

From this game on, whenever Arfield appeared in the starting line-up, it would usually be in this central midfield role; however, it would be revisionist to say that this caused a massive upturn in Rangers' performances for the remainder of this season. It did not, but it did help to illustrate the benefits of a central midfielder who was different from his peers. Someone who didn't have that exquisite close control or impressive ball retention, someone who was a little rough around the edges when in possession but capable of driving his team forward and impacting games in the final third.

Following the enforced early conclusion of 2019/20, Arfield's future was somewhat unknown. It was felt that his international exertions with Canada might be taking their toll on a player who struggled with injuries and consistency throughout those first two seasons. Reinforcements in attack with Kemar Roofe and Cedric Itten arriving to partner Morelos and the completion of Ianis Hagi's permanent transfer meant that consistent game time in the forward three would be unlikely. For a while, it looked like even a central midfield berth would escape his grasp, but as the 2020/21 season kicked into action, we would again see Gerrard and his coaching team further tweak and evolve the team's structure with remarkable effect.

Arfield made his first competitive start of the season in Rangers' 0-0 draw away to Livingston on 17 August 2020, playing in a midfield three with Jack and Kamara. The first points dropped of the campaign were not well received, and the midfield three's passive, safety-first style bore the brunt of the criticism, with Arfield himself being substituted in the 57th

POSITIONAL ROTATION

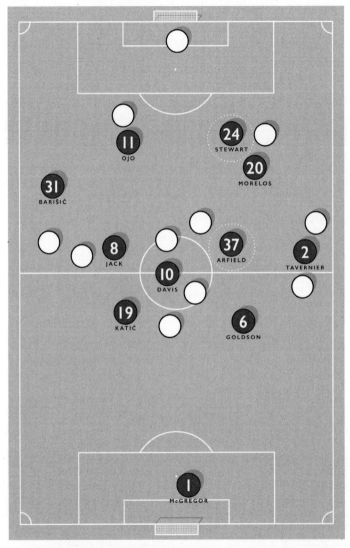

Rangers' increased use of positional rotations were a key factor in their new-found ability to break down defensive low blocks.

FIGURE 38

minute. In the next match, at home to Kilmarnock, Arfield found himself on the bench as Rangers switched back to a 4-2-3-1 formation with Jack and Steven Davis playing as a midfield two with four attackers ahead of them. In the subsequent games against Hamilton away and Dundee United at Ibrox, Arfield would play less than 60 minutes in total. There was a taste of things to come in his goalscoring second-half cameo against Dundee United as he replaced the injured Morelos on the hour mark and scored a fantastic goal, combining effortlessly with Hagi before breaking through to score.

He would repeat the trick another two times in his subsequent five appearances, with that aforementioned second goal against Hibs in a 2-2 draw – again combining with Hagi at the edge of the box and waltzing his way through to break the deadlock. Ten days later, he would do it again, scoring the first goal in the Europa League qualifying play-off round game against Galatasaray at Ibrox, following yet another one-two with the same player.

These goal examples display everything Rangers lacked in the year before: quick, vertical movement from deep in support of the attackers allied with some excellent one-touch combination play in advanced areas of the pitch.

This tactical concept is known as 'third man run' and is essential when breaking teams down. The third man run aims to utilise positional rotation, clever movement and creative passing with the sole purpose of finding an attacking player as they look to break the offside trap and run in behind the defence. This was an essential tool in Rangers' long-running search to break down stubborn teams and was a crucial part of their excellent form in the first half of season 2200/21.

Figure 39

The third man run is a combination between three players to free up one in space in an advantageous zone of the pitch. With player one in possession in the middle of the pitch, he has

THIRD MAN RUN

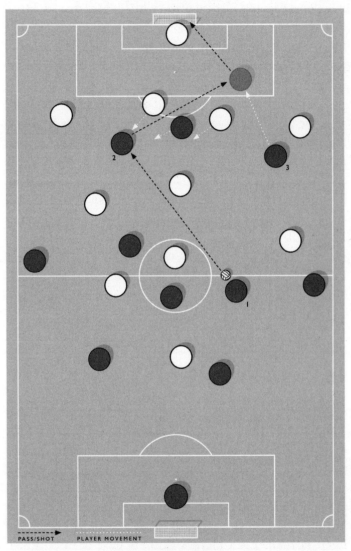

PASS/SHOT   PLAYER MOVEMENT

The third man run is a combination between three players to free up one of these players in space in an advantageous zone of the pitch.

FIGURE 39

various options to try and begin an attack, but most would result in a closed pass to a marked player with his back to goal. Player two will look to move deeper to receive the pass, thus dragging his marker out of position. Player one can then play a pass to player two at the same time as player three has left his marker and began to make a run through the opposition defence. Player two can then receive the ball, fend off his marker and quickly slide the ball in to player three, who is clean through on goal after breaking the offside trap. By forcing the defender to press player two, this opens the space which player three can fill. Still, the move requires a solid attacking structure to implement, quality and vision from the players involved and a high level of cohesion and understanding among attacking players to execute. Having the three players positioned on different vertical and horizontal lines is critical as this creates flexibility and can lead to confusion for the opposition. The third man run concept brings to life a key part of the coaching staff's 'occupy width and search for depth' principle.

Throughout the remainder of the championship-winning season, Rangers would enhance this further depending on the quality of opposition and availability of midfield personnel.

Figure 40

The midfield three of Kamara, Davis and Arfield was the most flexible and well-balanced choice and quickly became the default throughout autumn. The trio were a crucial component in Rangers rampaging into an unassailable lead in the title race and finishing unbeaten at the top of a Europa League group which contained Benfica, Standard Liege and Lech Poznań. Each player's skillsets have been outlined, but the balance and synchronicity all three brought to the midfield was the decisive factor. Davis was the conductor, dictating the tempo and probing his way through opposition lines of pressure. Kamara acted as the glue, knitting that left-hand side of the pitch together so effectively. Arfield was the

MIDFIELD FLEXIBILITY

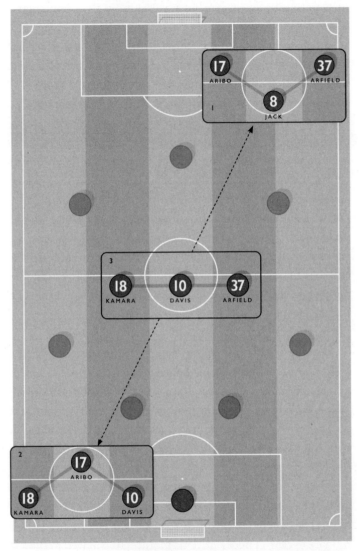

Kamara, Davis and Arfield represented the most balanced midfield three in the early months of season 20/21, but Rangers utilised other options effectively.

FIGURE 40

energy and chaos off the ball, tasked with taking the fight to teams and almost dragging his team up the pitch single-handedly on occasions.

If this three was the midfield of choice for the first half of the season, then Kamara, Davis and Joe Aribo were undoubtedly the main men in the engine room for the second half of the campaign. On 26 December, Arfield sustained an injury that would, unfortunately, keep him out of the team for eight games. With the injury to Ryan Jack and the less than impressive cameos by loan signing Bongani Zungu, Rangers were forced to turn to Aribo as their third central midfielder. Aribo arguably offered less than Arfield out of possession, but his ability on the ball and to create opportunities was undeniable. Playing Aribo in central midfield was perfect for those possession-heavy games where Rangers dominated the ball and his defensive deficiencies would not be exposed. On occasions where it was felt some additional support may be needed, Gerrard and Beale devised another tweak to ensure the midfield remained protected.

The next game following Rangers being declared league champions in March 2021 was against Celtic at Parkhead, which ended in a 1-1 draw. Rangers were without Tavernier, Jack and Arfield, meaning that all regular defensive support would not be available for Aribo on the right. Leon Balogun and Ianis Hagi started as right-back and right-sided attacker respectively and neither would describe this as their specialist position. Adding Aribo – who would say similar about central midfield – into the mix would create an imbalance to the right-sided structure out of possession, so Gerrard elected to switch Kamara to central midfield. This meant Aribo moved to the left where Ryan Kent and Borna Barišić could provide protection and give him the base to impose himself. This proved to be a wise move as in the early stages of the match, Celtic attacked down Rangers' right frequently, and Kamara's defensive nous and experience were hugely valuable.

It's tough to pick just one aspect of Aribo's style of play and use it to describe him. His languid, sock-down style is not automatically assumed to suit the Scottish leagues, but he became a crucial part of the team in his first three years at Rangers. His defensive work in the traditional sense of tracking runners and positioning himself to intercept counter-attacks was not at the level you would expect it to be as a central midfielder in this league. Still, he more than made up for it in other ways. One of his strongest skills in key games was his ability to use his excellent close control of the ball to keep possession in tight areas and give the team a breather.

For a player of his talent, he could and should have scored more goals throughout this period, but when he did score they tended to be quite spectacular.

Another option at this time was arguably the most attacking midfield three selection of them all. Ryan Jack Joe Aribo and Scott Arfield did not play together frequently but were selected to give Rangers a decisive win in a difficult away game in early November 2020. Rugby Park had been a bit of a graveyard for Rangers throughout Gerrard's time, but the new-found central attacking intent was again evident on this occasion. Jack played predominantly as the number six in this game, with Aribo and Arfield paired up as 'double free eights'. This was an incredibly bold attacking approach for the naturally cautious Gerrard, particularly in an away game, as Rangers started with just three nominally defensive players in Jack, Connor Goldson and Filip Helander. Rangers didn't exactly conjure up breathtaking attacking play during this stuffy 1-0 win courtesy of a Tavernier penalty, but they got the job done and gave the management team even more confidence that other combinations and skillsets in midfield could work and would continue to allow the team to play with the handbrake off in the majority of situations.

Whether Rangers played with a deeper midfield two and one attack-minded player, or whether they switched and utilised one holder and two free eights as against Kilmarnock, each game brought more flexibility and the evolution the coaching staff craved.

Throughout the title-winning season, Rangers successfully introduced creative attacking players into the centre of midfield who could assume the role of the magician that Michael Beale had outlined as important previously. This enhanced flexibility was crucial and, combined with maintaining an outstanding level of defensive consistency in the majority of their league games, was a huge contributing factor to the title triumph.

Twin Tens

'We've changed slightly the way we are playing, not a lot, probably the movement of five or ten yards with the two wide attackers, full-backs being a bit more adventurous.'

Michael Beale, The Scotsman

The number ten is probably the most iconic position on a football pitch, especially if like me you were an avid follower of Serie A during your formative years. Back then, every team seemed to have a number ten, whether it was Roberto Baggio, Alessandro Del Piero, Gianfranco Zola, Dennis Bergkamp or Rui Costa. There can, of course, be different variations. As football has evolved, stylistically different players such as Wayne Rooney and Marouane Fellaini would also play in the areas of the pitch we commonly associate with a number ten, despite their vastly differing skillsets.

But in its truest sense, the Italians call this role the *fantasista,* which sums up what the position means in a succinct yet expressive way.

The number ten is perhaps the one tactical role for which you can't immediately reel off a long list of Rangers greats. As a club, Rangers have been blessed with a host of legendary wingers and strikers and have a long-lasting love affair with goalkeepers, central defenders and traditional number eights.

Still, there are not too many who occupied this more advanced attacking midfield role and went on to greatness in a blue jersey. This can be explained in part as a by-product of the general tactical approach in Britain during this period. The number ten position was at its peak across Europe during the 1980s and '90s, at a time when the widely accepted tactical approach in Britain wasn't built to accommodate a player who played between the lines. Utilising a number ten who liked to drop deep and provide the link between midfield and attack would have meant adapting from a traditional 4-4-2 formation into something more complex and continental. This eventually came as the '90s progressed with Zola and Bergkamp leading the charge in England.

Ian Durrant, you could argue, had the skillset and quality to play in this position for Rangers and while he certainly did so on occasions, sadly, injuries robbed us for the most part of what was undoubtedly an exceptional talent. As tactics evolved in the late 1990s and Rangers sought to align the club more with the modern era, Ronald de Boer would perhaps be the closest in definition to the true number ten role, but the ex-Barcelona and Ajax attacker was past the peak of his powers when he arrived at Ibrox under Dick Advocaat. This was despite a fantastic season in 2002/03 as Rangers claimed the last of seven trebles in their history. De Boer was a player graced with incredible vision, poise and undoubted star quality but one who was undoubtedly a luxury attacker who could only be accommodated in a more modern continental set-up such as the one Advocaat created.

The increased importance in modern football of transitional attacking play dominated by pressing and counter-pressing has meant that teams cannot simply carry what came to be known as a luxury ball-player in the attacking third. Coupled with the rise of inverted wingers in the early to mid-2000s, this meant that, in essence, these players were occupying similar spaces to the number ten when cutting in on their stronger foot to create chances. With victory in the midfield battleground also becoming of crucial importance and therefore most teams electing to play a more solid and structured midfield three, this role as we knew it has been declining in popularity ever since.

For most of Gerrard's first season at Rangers, the front three comprised of Alfredo Morelos, Ryan Kent and Daniel Candeias in a 4-3-3 formation. The latter two players lined up primarily as orthodox wingers on the left and right respectively and were tasked with, in the case of Candeias, beating a man and firing crosses into the box. Kent, on the left, was equipped with much more of a modern skillset. A pacey wide attacker, Kent would use his two-footedness and explosive dribbling skills to beat his man on either side and create openings to attack. Given that Rangers were primarily a counter-attacking team who excelled at winning the ball back and attacking wide and fast in transition, it's fair to say that both players enjoyed a decent amount of success in 2018/19, finishing the season with a combined tally of 12 goals and 16 assists.

Candeias had arrived at the club in the summer of 2017 for £700,000 as part of the ill-fated Pedro Caixinha's reign. He was a player the Portuguese manager clearly trusted, having managed him earlier in his career. Candeias was what is now classed as a traditional right-winger; his primary intention was always to attack his full-back and whip crosses into the box. Candeias possessed searing pace and an extraordinary work ethic, but in many ways, he summed up Rangers during that first season, capable of brilliance on his day but consistent top-level quality was lacking overall. Despite that, he contributed to 16 goals in his second and final season at the club, linking very well with right-sided partner James Tavernier.

One thing that was not inconsistent about Candeias was his outstanding work when out of possession, something you wouldn't typically associate with an attacking player, never mind a winger. In fact, there is an argument that his role at Rangers could be classed as a 'defensive winger' whose primary job was to provide the base on which Tavernier's attacking talents were allowed to flourish.

The two seemed to work telepathically as a partnership at times, with both players flexible enough to interchange fluidly as and when the scenario demanded it to cause maximum damage to the opposition. In a 5-0 victory against Kilmarnock in the Scottish Cup in February 2019, Candeias finished the match with three assists. Two of these perfectly encapsulate the main attacking attributes associated with the winger's game.

In this first example, Candeias showcased that combination play with Tavernier by using his positional intelligence and speed to create an attacking opportunity. Tavernier won the ball back in his half to thwart a counter-attack and drove forward at pace. Candeias pulled wide in anticipation of receiving a ball on the flank and stretching play but instead elected to sprint round the defender on his blind side to beat the offside trap at the last second. Tavernier played an inch-perfect through pass between the centre-back and left-back, leaving Candeias in acres of space to roll the ball across goal for Alfredo Morelos to finish from inside the box.

Figure 41

In the second example, Tavernier and Candeias utilised positional rotation to create a different type of chance, with the same outcome: another Morelos goal. Tavernier picked the ball up wide on the touchline, with Candeias inside being marked by two Kilmarnock defenders. Candeias attempted to create space and draw the defenders out by running around Tavernier, but as he continued his run on the outside this gave him a yard of space while the defenders readjusted. This split second allowed Tavernier to play the ball to Candeias down the flank, who was then able to whip an excellent cross into the six-yard box for Morelos to head home.

The third assist in this game is slightly different and instead of Candeias's ability on the ball this was more about showcasing

CANDEIAS WING PLAY

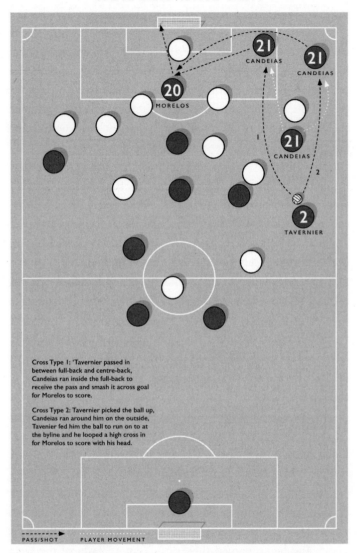

Cross Type 1: 'Tavernier passed in between full-back and centre-back, Candeias ran inside the full-back to receive the pass and smash it across goal for Morelos to score.

Cross Type 2: Tavernier picked the ball up, Candeias ran around him on the outside, Tavenier fed him the ball to run on to at the byline and he looped a high cross in for Morelos to score with his head.

In season 2018/19, Candeias's ability both on and off the ball was crucial for Rangers.

FIGURE 41

his excellent pressing ability and tenacity to recover loose balls. Rangers looked to counter through Tavernier, who played a quick vertical ball into Candeias's feet. Candeias was unable to control the pass and lost possession of the ball, and the chance looked to be gone. With assistance from Ryan Jack, Candeias counter-pressed to hunt down the Kilmarnock midfielder, picked his pocket and retained possession. Candeias ushered the ball forward to Morelos, who carried it into the box and finished for his hat-trick in one sweeping motion.

In many ways, his unrelenting work rate and attitude were symbolic of Gerrard's team during this first season. Lacking consistency on the ball quality at times, but with a fighting spirit that ensured on their day, they could go toe to toe with any team they faced. In the 3-1 victory against Rapid Vienna in the Europa League group stage in September 2018, we saw a prime example of this as Candeias cleared a corner on the edge of his area and raced upfield to battle with the defender to contest his own clearance. His tenacity paid off, and he could skilfully back-heel the ball through to Morelos, who advanced on goal. He scored the third to give Rangers victory in their first Europa League group game since returning to the top division.

In 21-year-old Ryan Kent, Rangers recruited a player who Michael Beale had worked closely with during his time in Liverpool's youth academies. Kent had been heavily linked with Rangers throughout that first summer before finally joining on loan on 22 July 2018. A player of immense potential, Kent immediately slotted in on the left of the attack and made a vital contribution to the season, finishing with six goals and six assists and being named the SPFL Young Player of the Year. His direct dribbling style, ability to beat his man on either foot and outstanding aggression and intensity when out of possession ensured that he quickly became a player the fans would look for to provide excitement and a spark in games, despite his relatively young age. In his first season, Kent also performed very well in the majority of the Old Firm matches – an essential proving ground for any successful Ranger – particularly the 2018 new year fixture where he gave Celtic right-back Mikael Lustig a torrid time. Kent would turn him inside out down the left flank more times than he would like to remember but most notably when creating the only goal of the game, scored by Ryan Jack.

Figure 42

This goal neatly sums up Kent's traditional wing play in the first season as he picked the ball up on the touchline deep in his half. Andy Halliday, playing as a converted left-back, would not be a player you would associate with lung-bursting runs on the overlap; therefore, it would be Kent's responsibility to advance with the ball and create danger himself.

As play progressed into the Celtic defensive third, Kent was able to isolate Lustig in a dangerous area of the pitch and created a one vs one opportunity. On this occasion, Kent elected to utilise his pace and hit the byline before dummying a cross across goal, which Lustig failed to read. Instead, Kent cut the ball back into the penalty area and found Jack arriving in the box, who gave Rangers the lead and their first victory over Celtic in 13 games.

While Kent was classed as a traditional winger, his role would be substantially more complex than that of Candeias. Not renowned for his crossing ability, Kent would instead rely on his pace and two-footed ability to commit his man and force opportunities for himself or his team-mates. Such is his close control and quality on the ball, Kent was a crucial player for Rangers in the final third and would go on to evolve into a modern pressing forward.

Kent would also score his first Old Firm goal that season, the consolation in the third derby, but this strike was all about showcasing his strength on the ball as he held off two defenders and burst through the middle to score at Parkhead. Kent playing in a more central role was undoubtedly an exciting prospect,

KENT WING PLAY IN SEASON ONE
Rangers 1 - 0 Celtic SPFL 29.12.18

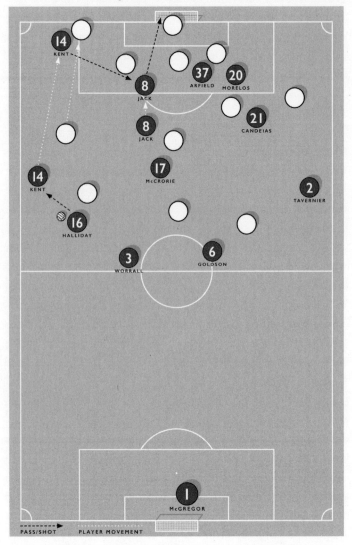

Ryan Kent was used as a classic left-winger for most of his first season at the club.

FIGURE 42

and with hindsight, this goal could have been seen as a taste of things to come.

On the last day of March, Rangers succumbed to a disappointing 2-1 defeat at the hands of Celtic courtesy of a late James Forrest goal which all but put to bed their title challenge for another year. But disappointment is the nurse of wisdom, as they say. Alfredo Morelos was sent off again and would miss four games as a result. The absence of Morelos would be a vital factor – whether by accident or design – in what soon became known as the first major tactical shift of the Gerrard era.

Figure 43

His replacement in the team was January signing Jermain Defoe, not a bad alternative even at 36 years old but certainly not comparable to Morelos's all-action physical style. A shift in tactical approach was therefore deemed necessary to provide support to Defoe, who was still a supreme goalscorer but had never been as adept at dropping deep to link play as his Colombian counterpart. Defoe was a number nine, much more comfortable playing off the shoulder of the defence and doing his best work in the penalty area.

Rangers' style of getting the ball wide and crossing into the box was therefore deemed to be as effective a route to goal, and as such, they needed to provide Defoe with the platform to succeed. To do this, Rangers asked their wide players to play as 'inside tens' and nominally position themselves ten yards infield from the flanks in the left and right half-spaces. Scott Arfield, a more natural central player replaced Candeias, with Kent remaining as the team's left-sided attacker to aid with this evolution. The idea was that Arfield and Kent would link better with Defoe from this starting position and form a tight three-pronged attack.

Another key benefit of this approach was increased numbers in central areas which would aid with overloading the opposition defence by taking advantage of space between opposition full-

THE FRONT THREE

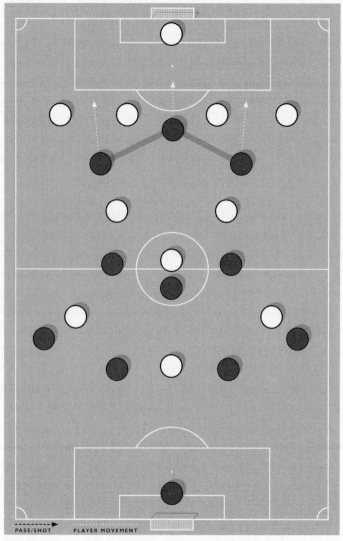

PASS/SHOT   PLAYER MOVEMENT

Switching to a front three allowed Rangers to overload more effectively and take advantage of space between full-backs and centre-backs.

FIGURE 43

backs and centre-backs. This helped in offensive situations but also with winning the ball back higher up the field, as this could turn defensive situations into attacking ones.

Rangers would win their next six games in a row, including a 2-0 victory against Celtic at Parkhead, which showcased their budding attacking approach to its fullest.

Figure 44

Jon Flanagan had the ball on the left-hand touchline and moved it to Glen Kamara, who was now in his customary left central midfield position. Kamara swivelled his hips to glide past the first Celtic challenge and advance into the middle of the park. Note the position of Kent, in the centre of the pitch far away from the left flank, a situation that would go on to become something of a regular occurrence in this fixture.

As Kamara progressed into the box, the second number ten, Scott Arfield, was in an advanced position providing that support to Defoe.

Kamara played a simple ball into the feet of Defoe, who employed an exquisite dummy to utterly wrong-foot the Celtic defence.

Arfield gambled on going beyond the defence by making that trademark third man run, received the ball and slid it past the on-rushing goalkeeper to give Rangers a 2-0 lead and back-to-back home wins against Celtic.

Coincidentally, Morelos returned to the team for Rangers' final game of the season, a 2-1 defeat away to Kilmarnock, where the Colombian would score his 30th goal of a very eventful campaign on a personal level. But regardless of that and another failed league campaign, the mood was still optimistic going into the new season. The incremental improvements in both the tactical set-up and the player quality being brought to the club in the winter and summer of 2019 helped to ensure Rangers were not quite as one-dimensional as they had been previously. Their attacking play had been focused down the

TWIN TENS IN ACTION
Rangers 2-0 Celtic SPFL 12.05.19

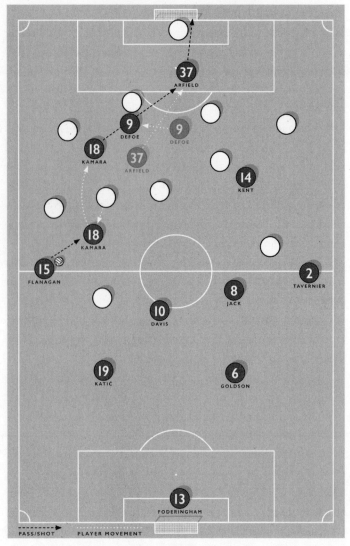

The switch to twin number tens allowed Rangers to attack areas of the pitch that previously
had not been possible when playing with traditional wingers.

FIGURE 44

wings throughout the league campaign, and attacks would essentially be in isolation. Crosses into the box were usually the order of the day, which would either find the target or be headed clear to try again.

This tweak to use 'twin tens' gave Rangers more territorial advantage in the half-spaces and allowed the team to utilise positional rotation in these areas to create gaps in the opposition defensive structure. The result was that the team had central midfielders and number tens starting in higher positions on the field during an opposing defensive build-up. Should a Rangers attack break down and the ball be cleared, the positioning of these players was such that it would allow the team to keep the pressure on and layer their attacks to suffocate teams in the defensive third.

When you consider that the introduction of the flat midfield three occurred during the same run of games at the end of that first season, it was evident that the management team had discovered an approach that gave Rangers a more fluid and flexible attack. Better yet, they had also managed to maintain – and even improve – the defensive structure that Gerrard had worked so hard to implement in the early months of that debut season.

Following Kent's return on a permanent deal, he would continue to predominantly play as the left-sided number ten in the front three throughout the next two seasons. There was a concern that asking Kent to play as a narrower attacker would diminish his more traditional tendencies on the wing; however, the opposite proved to be true. From a starting position on the left, a winger's abilities are automatically limited due to the physical constraints of the touchline. At times in his first season Kent could appear one-dimensional and as a result of this he was always looking to cut in on his right to attack centrally. By changing his starting position to a more central area of the pitch where he could utilise his dynamism to cause maximum impact in the final third, Kent looked to be unleashed. In the early months of 2020/21 he was the form player in the league as he started to come into his own as an elite attacker at that level. With the narrow front three supported by the better-structured midfield three, Kent could reap the benefits of a higher starting position to impact the game in much more dangerous areas of the pitch without necessarily having to worry about tracking back to protect his full-back.

There were inconsistencies, as there are with all flair players, but the key aspect that marks Kent out from his peers is when he isn't playing as well as he can he still has that phenomenal work rate when out of possession. His ability to track back and pressure opponents was unrivalled and almost as vital a weapon in Europe as his pace on the counter-attack. Against Braga in the 2020/21 Europa League last 32, Kent's pace on the break was vital in ensuring Rangers progressed into the last 16 as he pounced on a terrific defence-splitting pass by Hagi and broke through to finish past the keeper. Similar to his goal at Parkhead a year earlier, this was somewhat of a trademark goal of Kent's as he used that fantastic off-ball movement coupled with pace and close control to devastating effect.

At times, Kent could give the impression of trying to force attacks, either due to poor performance or his desire to be the primary creator for the team, but his attitude and application were rarely in question.

Towards the end of the title-winning season, we would see another evolution in Kent's role as – primarily in games against Celtic – he would be utilised as a sole number ten playing behind two central strikers. This move further emphasised Kent's abilities in the critical, creative area of the pitch and his performances in these games showcased a potential future evolution for the team. Playing in this role, Kent was not only able to influence games but he was also able to use that pace and ability out of possession to impact Celtic's build-up play through their defensive midfielders, thus creating opportunities for Rangers to counter-press. This was showcased in two fantastic performances in the Old Firm derby at the tail end of the season with the first coming in a 2-0 Scottish Cup victory in mid-April and the latter a virtuoso man of the match performance in Rangers' 4-1 league victory in early May 2021.

Steven Gerrard had been constantly searching for ways to get more firepower into the team, and towards the end of this season he appeared to have settled on a partnership of Morelos and Roofe with Kent playing in behind as the sole number ten in a 4-3-1-2 formation. In that double header against Celtic, as outlined on the page across, Kent's tactical role was twofold. Firstly, it was his job to get on the ball in the centre of the pitch and direct attacks down the wings or attack centrally himself using combination play with Morelos and Roofe. The secondary aspect of this role was to man-mark Celtic's deepest midfielder, Scott Brown. By pressing the ageing Brown, Kent was able to block the Celtic build-up play effectively and force their defenders into mistakes in deep areas or to attempt long passes frpm which Rangers could recover easily. It was a tactic that worked to terrific effect and showcased the evolution of Kent since his first season at the club.

Figure 45

With the departure of Candeias and while awaiting the re-signing of Kent, the most prominent players in the number ten positions during the early weeks and months of 2019/20 were Arfield and new signings Sheyi Ojo and Jordan Jones.

Like Kent the previous season, Ojo had arrived on loan from Liverpool with the coaching staff and scouting network making good use of their previous relationships and intrinsic knowledge of the club's academy players. Despite weighing in with five goals and five assists before COVID curtailed the season early, Ojo would unfortunately not have the same long-lasting impact as Kent did. The youngster will be remembered fondly for scoring the only goal as Rangers beat Feyenoord 1-0 at Ibrox in the group stages of that season's Europa League.

RYAN KENT EVOLUTION

Ryan Kent's evolution would continue towards the end of season 2020/21, with a move to central number ten proving successful in two quickfire victories against Celtic.

FIGURE 45

Jones enjoyed a promising start to the campaign, including a starring role against FC Midtjylland in the Europa League third qualifying round. Rangers utilised his searing pace on the break to significant effect throughout to win the first leg 4-2 and all but seal their passage into the final round.

Both players – along with Greg Stewart and Brandon Barker – were signed to provide competition in the two supporting slots behind Morelos; however, not all of them seemed to fit the new tactical style the management team were in the process of implementing. Jones and Barker, in particular, were predominantly inverted wingers or inside-forwards who liked to utilise their pace to either run at defenders on the flank or to find gaps behind opposition defensive lines. This was an incredibly useful tactic when playing for teams like Kilmarnock and Hibs but playing against packed defences at Rangers and being asked to play intricate passing moves in central areas wasn't something that either player ever looked entirely comfortable with. Arguably Stewart was the player who did fit best with this new number ten approach and he would go on to showcase some ability in patches during the rare appearances he was offered.

As the 2019/20 season progressed, it was clear that the position on the right vacated by Candeias required some additional consideration if this was to prove as fruitful as the switch to a number ten had been for Kent.

Hybrid Attackers

'We have a couple of players who are capable of dropping down and playing as hybrids if you like. But it is an area where, last year, come the end of the season with the volume of games, we felt we were short at times.'

Steven Gerrard, The Herald, *18 August 2021*

Positional rotation is a phrase that has entered the footballing lexicon more and more over the last few years. It's not a new concept; there aren't many of them still about, it's quite the opposite. In fact the term originates – like most things in the modern game – from the Dutch school of Total Football made famous in the early 1970s by Rinus Michaels and Johan Cruyff. The contemporary evolution of this footballing philosophy has become known as 'Juego de Posición', which translates to English as 'positional play' and was, of course, re-popularised at Barcelona by Cruyff's most famous disciple, Pep Guardiola.

Most present-day teams are influenced in at least some way by positional play, given how all-encompassing and far-reaching it has become, but it is precisely the rotational aspect that Rangers managed to successfully integrate during their second and third seasons under Gerrard. In a previous chapter, Rangers' use of such rotations in central midfield to create space to attack was illustrated primarily through Scott Arfield's ability to make third runs beyond the team forward line into gaps left in the opposition defensive line. The idea of positional rotation through the middle and attacking thirds of the pitch has become much more commonplace throughout football over the last ten years. The aim is to offer support to the player in possession while also advancing the ball behind the opposition's defensive line.

As the search for superiority on the pitch becomes ever more fraught, coaches are constantly trying to achieve this in more creative or uncommon ways. One such method is through the use of players who are often described as 'hybrids'.

In its very essence, a hybrid is described as 'a thing made by combining two different elements'. In football parlance, this can be an adjective to describe a player with a varied enough skillset to be utilised in multiple game scenarios and areas of the pitch. It is worth remembering the differences between a player's position and the tactical role they are asked to fulfil within a team structure. The skillset of Daniel Candeias, when asked to play in the right-sided attacker role at Rangers, is very different to the expertise of both Ianis Hagi and Joe Aribo and considerably different again to what Kemar Roofe brought to the position. Football is no longer constrained to specific types of players who play the position in the same way as everyone. Flexibility is king.

As we have established throughout, this Rangers team was remarkably well-drilled, with clear and continued focus placed on repetition of patterns of play and the importance of defensive structure. You could predict between seven and nine starters throughout the title-winning season on any given matchday, usually on the higher side of that range. Consistency and success tend to go hand in hand for most title-winning football teams, but this can sometimes lead to predictability and staleness. Football teams need magic, players who get fans off their seats to marvel at off-the-cuff brilliance. Rangers introduced flexibility into the midfield three in season 2020/21 but, allied to that, was the replacement of Candeias with a combination of hybrid players in the two wide attacking roles in support of Alfredo Morelos.

Figure 46

As one of the team's most consistent and available players, Ryan Kent would always play if fit and, more often than not, find himself starting as the left-sided number ten. There were specific scenarios where he may roam and find himself almost in a free role, but generally speaking he would begin matches in that area of the pitch. It was a similar story for Glen Kamara; in most games, he would line up as the left-sided central midfielder in a middle three unless specific balance – to counter an opponent or provide support to a certain team-mate – was required on the opposite side. That generally left two roles in the team that could be classed as truly hybrid, as they changed from game to game depending on the player selected or the specific situation: the right-sided central midfielder and the right-sided number ten.

Ex-Charlton attacking midfielder Joe Aribo signed in the summer of 2019 ahead of Gerrard's second season in charge. Billed as a modern number ten before his arrival, he rarely played this role for Rangers in his first two seasons. Aribo would epitomise a hybrid player's unexpected and unconventional nature by regularly appearing in both left and right central midfield roles and any of the three attacking midfield spots, should the approach for a game require it. He was an enigma within Scottish football, capable of conjuring inexplicable moments of brilliance on the pitch, all the while never seeming entirely in control of his subsequent actions or thoughts.

When you first see Aribo, you would not guess that his physical profile – he is 6ft 2in with an athletic frame akin to a boxer – would produce such a gifted, light-footed technical footballer. Blessed with extreme talent in his feet, Aribo tended to glide around the pitch. When played in the right-sided number ten role – which he occupied more often in his first

THE HYBRID POSITIONS

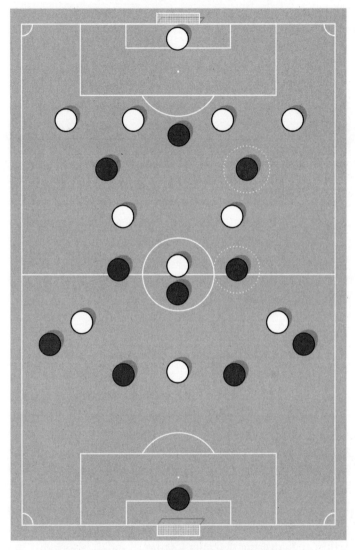

Rangers' use of 'hybrid' players would add some much-needed unpredictability to such a well-structured tactical framework.

FIGURE 46

season – he had all the hallmarks of an 'inverted winger', a player who plays nominally in a position usually reserved for a winger but is anything but. The skillset required for this role matches Aribo perfectly as he does not display any characteristics of a classic winger and equally isn't a player who will cut inside and look to find an opening to score in the way that an inverted forward such as Arjen Robben would look to do. As Aribo is predominantly left-footed, when the coaching staff elected to use him on the right in this inverted way, it provided another layer to how Rangers could build their attacks.

Playing wider as the right-sided ten allows him to cut inside into the half-space and attack opposition teams at one of the weakest points in their defensive structure. Given the majority of centre-backs are still right-footed, it's generally accepted that the space between the left centre-back and the left-back is prime to exploit as both players are forced to use their weaker foot to defend in this area.

Figure 47

If you were to select a signature Aribo goal it would be in the 5-0 win against Ross County at Ibrox on 21 January 2021, where he supplied a sumptuous finish to make it 3-0 just before half-time. Picking the ball up in the right-hand channel from Tavernier, he took it to the byline before facing up to Charlie Lakin. Ordinarily, a player in this situation would look to navigate their way into the box using combination play with a forward, or possibly look to find space to cross into the box. But, given the type of footballer Aribo is, and using that aforementioned ball control, he instead slalomed past both Lakin and covering defender Connor Randall before shifting his weight to find a yard of space to curl a left-footed shot into the far corner of the net. It was an incredible finish and showcased precisely what Aribo can bring in that attacking role against teams who will come to Ibrox content to sit deep and spoil play.

ARIBO - THE INVERTED WINGER
Rangers 5-0 Ross County SPFL 31.01.21

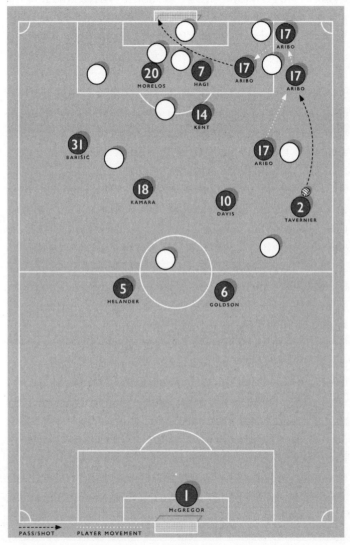

Aribo receives the pass from Tavernier on the right flank, jinks onto his left foot past two challenges and curls the ball into the far corner of the keeper's net.

FIGURE 47

227

This further shows how the right-sided attacker role has evolved throughout the three years under Gerrard and how the player relationships have developed. Aribo linked very well with James Tavernier and Nathan Patterson on the right, with both players capable of playing narrow or wide, should the situation demand it. Indeed, at times in games – most memorably the 2-0 Scottish Cup win against Celtic in April 2021 – Aribo essentially played as a 'chalk on the boots' winger wide on the right touchline. This allowed Rangers to stretch Celtic's defence and allow Patterson and Arfield the space to cause an impact centrally with their direct vertical runs through the half-space.

Throughout many interviews, Michael Beale referenced his love for players who can receive the ball on the half-turn and use their 'Action Man hips' as a way to beat their man sometimes even before they touch the ball. Aribo has this quality in abundance, as does his sometime midfield partner and close friend Glen Kamara. When Aribo played in central midfield, as he did more often in the title-winning season, there is an argument that Rangers naturally lose some defensive strength, certainly compared to the previous season with the flat midfield three of Jack, Davis and Kamara. Given Aribo's skillset, it is understandable that tracking runners and covering space was not a natural facet of his game but the general consensus was that the additional creativity and ball-carrying ability was deemed of a higher priority in certain occasions. Along with Kent, Aribo was the most natural dribbler at the club during the championship-winning season, and playing in central midfield afforded him the time and space to use this to maximum effect. This proved very successful for Rangers in those stuffy games against teams playing low blocks, as someone who can carry the ball at speed and beat their opponent at will is a key factor in creating and taking advantage of any gaps that may appear. In his mid-20s, Aribo still has some time to develop his game further, and the one area he could improve on would be his final ball and efficiency in front of goal. Given his outstanding close control and physical ability, he still tended to overplay at times and miss opportunities to create for his team-mates in dangerous areas. Also not famed as a player who was clinical in front of goal or blessed with long-distance shooting accuracy, he can take his game to the next level if he can harness this effectively and be decisive in and around the penalty area.

Such was his undoubted flexibility – a key component of Rangers' tactical philosophy – it was also not uncommon to see Aribo fill in as an emergency left-back, most memorably in the Europa League round of 32 first leg at Ibrox against Braga in February 2020. His introduction contributed to a magnificent comeback from Rangers to win the game, having trailed Braga by two goals after 60 minutes. Aribo replaced Kamara in the second half, but an injury to Borna Barišić saw him shifted to left-back and he was again tasked with providing attacking impetus in an unfamiliar and much deeper role.

In one of the most exhilarating nights of football Ibrox has seen for many a year, this change was arguably the decisive factor in the game. Rangers struggled badly to contain a very slick Braga team who were adept at stretching Rangers' usually sound defensive structure. Indeed, Rangers could and should have been losing by more than 2-0 before the change was made. The introduction of Aribo at left-back gave Rangers another dimension to attack and they used this to terrific effect in the 75th minute to bring the game back to 2-2.

Aribo won the ball back on the left touchline and played a one-two with Ianis Hagi into the centre of the pitch. As he picked up the return pass, he faced up to two lines of opposition defenders tightly marking Rangers' attacking players. Displaying the level of confidence and exquisite close control he would become known for, he jinked his way past four or five defenders in the most chaotic yet controlled way. This sequence felt like a sleight of hand trick as Aribo appeared to be the only person in the stadium who knew where the ball was at all times. When he eventually broke free of the defence, he found himself bearing down on goal and all that was left to do was calmly pass the ball past Braga goalkeeper Matheus to send Ibrox into bedlam. It was an unbelievable goal and a moment of brilliance from the Nigerian that will be remembered for years to come, particularly given Rangers would go on to win the game and progress into the last 16.

Figure 48

Aribo was again asked to play as a left-back in the last two games of the title-winning season in May 2021, a 3-0 away victory against Livingston and trophy day itself, the 4-0 win against Aberdeen at Ibrox. Despite these games being uncompetitive due to Rangers wrapping the title up two months prior, Steven Gerrard told Rangers TV between these two fixtures, 'What can I say about Joe Aribo? I'll tell you what I'll say about him: good players can play football, top players can play anywhere.

'A manager can ask a player to do a role, and good players can do some, and good players can't do some – but Joe Aribo is a top player. Whatever I ask him to do, he goes out and gives it his best shot.

'He's my man of the match tonight just because, if you think about it, he's a number ten. That left-back performance is as good as we've seen in my three years of being here. So well done to him for parking his ego and doing a job for his team-mates.'

Good players can play anywhere, as Aribo nicely outlines. Having played in five different positions in just two years at Rangers, he is a proper hybrid footballer and a symbol of the team's flexibility that brought such success.

In Ianis Hagi, Rangers have a player who frequently plays in the same positions as Aribo but has an entirely different skillset. When the young Romanian joined on loan from Belgian club Genk, the initial discussions about his suitability were focused on whether he was capable of playing as a twin ten. Some fans believed that he had to be used as a central number ten to make up for his lack of pace and allow him to shine in optimum areas

JOE ARIBO – THE HYBRID FOOTBALLER

Rangers 3-2 SC Braga Europa League 20.02.20

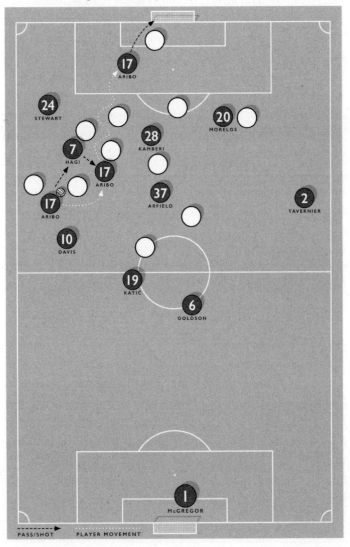

Aribo was a symbol of the team's flexibility, playing in five different positions in his first two years at the club.

FIGURE 48

of the pitch. Hagi's work off the ball is very under-rated for a perceived 'luxury' player. His ability to press and counter-press created some high-quality opportunities for Rangers throughout his first two seasons under Gerrard. Hagi has a mentality that belies his years and arguably isn't associated with this type of flair or luxury player. As with Aribo, the Romanian is a prime example of the 'You vs Yourself mentality' that Gerrard and the coaching staff implemented, with the player constantly looking to improve himself and willing to play anywhere for the good of the team.

Hagi signed in the January 2020 window, and it is not untrue to say that the then 21-year-old proved to be an absolute breath of fresh air as Rangers found themselves in another difficult post-winter break period. On his full debut, he would score the winner in a scrappy 2-1 victory against Hibs at Ibrox, which not only gave Rangers their first win in three league games, it would showcase just what fans could expect from the gifted young attacker.

With just six minutes left on the clock and Rangers drawing 1-1, yet another corner was cleared by Hibs to the edge of the area. Scott Arfield headed the ball back into the box to attempt to maintain the pressure on their defensive third, and as Goldson flicked the ball on, Hagi came alive and gambled with his movement at the back post. With the Hibs defence caught advancing, they were in no man's land as the ball made its way to Hagi, who let it bounce across himself before contorting his body to connect perfectly with his right foot and half-volley the ball back across goal and into the bottom-left corner. An incredibly difficult technique to get right at any time, but at that stage of the game and on your debut, it was all the more impressive.

In many ways, he is the antithesis to Aribo. Hagi arguably doesn't have an exceptionally expansive passing range and isn't as renowned a ball carrier, given he isn't blessed with any kind of burst of pace even over shorter distances. Quite simply, Hagi just made things happen on a football pitch. He has a consistent coolness in his veins in decisive moments that not many other players have in the final third and certainly not one at such a young age. His essential skills are his quickness of mind and that innate vision that all good number tens have to see the picture before it's painted.

His ability with both feet – coaches who have worked with him in the past were noted as genuinely unable to decide which foot he was more comfortable using – helped to distinguish him from his peers. When he receives the ball in the attacking third, he can beat opponents comfortably on both sides and create chances from angles that others would find impossible. His first goal against Braga, when compared to that debut goal against Hibs, showcases just how flexible he can be. Picking the ball up in the same area of the pitch, Hagi shifted on to his left foot this time and cut inside the defender before unleashing another unstoppable finish into the right-hand corner.

Figure 49

In the 18 months from that debut against Hibs in February 2020 until his final appearance of 2020/21 in the 4-0 win against Aberdeen at Ibrox, Hagi scored or assisted 25 goals in just 59 appearances. For all Arfield gets the glory for his ability to run off the ball and make those third man runs to break teams down and score goals, it was nearly always Hagi who played the crucial second pass through the lines for him to break through and finish. He is not the type of player who will dominate a game from start to finish as Alfredo Morelos would do, but Hagi consistently delivers in key moments in games in a way that few others within the squad can do. He finished 2020/21 with the most assists in the league, which is impressive considering his age, but equally so given he was not always guaranteed a first-team place.

Hagi's vision and decisive ability on the ball was so valuable for Rangers and was on show once again in the return leg against

HAGI — THE HYBRID
Rangers 3-2 SC Braga Europa League 20.02.20

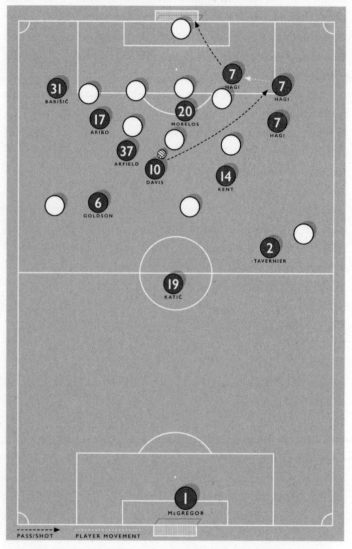

PASS/SHOT   PLAYER MOVEMENT

Hagi's ability with either foot allowed him to impact the game from all across the attacking third of the pitch.

FIGURE 49

Braga. In a tight game which Rangers won 1-0, the moment of magic came from Hagi as it so often did. Picking the ball up in his own half, he delivered a delightful defence-splitting pass for Kent to break the Braga offside trap and score the only goal of the game to send Rangers through to the last 16 of the Europa League for the first time in 12 years.

Figure 50

Like Aribo, Hagi has been used deeper at times – albeit not anywhere near as often – as a 'free eight' in the 4-3-3 system and again brought a different skillset to the role, using his ability off the ball and vision from deep. This pliability in terms of his role on the pitch again marks him out as a hybrid player capable of playing in many different positions.

The final hybrid player was Kemar Roofe, as the ex-Oxford and Leeds forward was added to the squad in the summer 2020 transfer window. This signing was a significant coup as the Englishman was seen as the player to finally offer the additional firepower that was badly needed to support Alfredo Morelos. Almost immediately Roofe's hybrid qualities would become apparent. For most people, Roofe is perhaps an odd choice for a hybrid player; however, throughout 2020/21 he displayed some classic traits of the genre. Rangers had a lot of high potential who were close to but not quite yet at their peak within the squad, such as Kent, Morelos and Hagi, and they had experienced veterans like Steven Davis, Scott Arfield and Jermain Defoe. In their quest for the league title, they badly craved 'win now' players such as Roofe, who were coming into their prime and ready to significantly impact the first team.

In the season prior, as outlined Rangers primarily used Aribo or Hagi in the right-sided attacker role as both had different skillsets that would allow flexibility in that position should the game demand it. Roofe was different; he added goals, the one thing this team badly needed. With Kent's role primarily as a dribbler and creator on the left-hand side – and the enormous

IANIS HAGI – VISION
SC Braga 0-1 Rangers Europa League 26.02.20

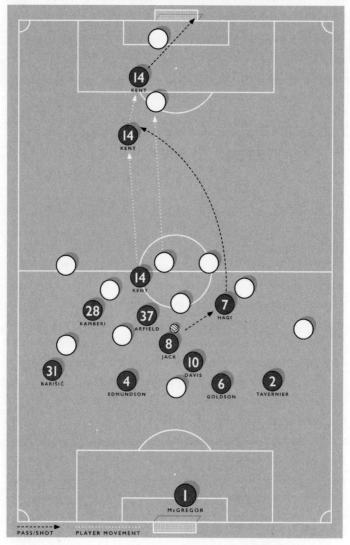

PASS/SHOT   PLAYER MOVEMENT

Ianis Hagi's vision was evident from the early months of his loan signing and would become a vital part of Rangers' success.

FIGURE 50

236

attacking role James Tavernier plays in the final third on the right – there was definitely space for a player who could position themselves higher up the pitch in certain in-game scenarios and add another means of firepower in dangerous areas.

Despite Morelos's goalscoring exploits during his two years before Roofe joined, the Colombian was prone to purple patches of scoring, and when the goals dried up, they were in drastically short supply from other areas. In Roofe's debut season, despite all-too-regular and frustrating periods out of the team injured, he finished as the top scorer with 19 goals in all competitions, just one ahead of Morelos. Having another player in the attacking areas who can contribute goals was hugely welcome. This gave the team another dimension to their attack and encouraged them to be less predictable in their build-up play.

Roofe was a rare breed in this Rangers side, a number nine who rarely played as a number nine. From Daniel Candeias occupying that role just 18 months previous, Rangers had undergone a complete evolution in this area of the pitch. They had given themselves the option of playing two strikers should the situation require it, but still within the tactical structure the coaching team had worked so hard to implement. The results proved quite fruitful as the opportunity to rotate both Roofe and Morelos throughout those taxing winter months proved invaluable. As with the story of each season under Gerrard, comparisons before Christmas and after Christmas proved pretty insightful, but, in this instance both are thankfully happy comparisons.

Both players can be stylistically similar in some respects, albeit Roofe doesn't have the physical profile of Morelos, and this bears out when watching them on the pitch. Both do like to come deep and link play at times, but Morelos is much more all-action, preferring to take the ball in with his back to goal and drag defenders with him to create openings in behind.

Roofe could be seen as more of a penalty area player, constantly on the move in the box looking to sniff out any half-chances that may present themselves to him. He was also surprisingly adept with his head when given the space and time, as he showed memorably with a headed goal where he seemed to hang in the air for an eternity in the 4-1 victory against Celtic in May 2021. He will also be fondly remembered for THAT goal against Standard Liege in October 2020 as he picked the ball up late in the game, promptly beat three men and scored from still inside his own half to seal Rangers' 2-0 victory in the Europa League group stage. It was an incredible goal seen around the continent that night and summed up the confidence Roofe had in his abilities on the football pitch. At times during those dark and cold November and December days, that glamour seemed very far away but Roofe was still there plugging away. It felt like Roofe was carrying the team on his own during this period as he scored nine goals in just 11 games in a crucial period in which Rangers accelerated away from a combusting Celtic team to take pole position in the title race. Injuries and physical capability were always an issue for Roofe but one thing was for sure – if the ball broke to any Rangers player in the box when the chips were down and a goal was needed, he was the one who could be counted on to put the chance away.

Alfredo Morelos Evolution

'You will always have to live with the genius – the genius will not live with you. I keep hearing people in football talking about everybody being treated the same. They are lying. The majority of guys in a football dressing room know that the ones who are the exceptional players will be allowed a bit of laxity.

'With Gascoigne, I had to sit down with the whole dressing room and tell them, "This is what we have here. We have a boy who will win us games. So we all have to handle him."'

Walter Smith on Gazza

Each section leading up until this point has described the position or tactical role within the team and used the specific talents of certain players to chart team and player evolution. Sometimes, a manager just happens to find themselves with a talent that transcends any tactical role you could try to place upon them.

Alfredo Morelos's path to Rangers is well known by now, joining the club as a precocious 21-year-old following a whirlwind goal-laden 18 months playing in the Veikkausliiga with HJK Helsinki. During his time in Finland, Rangers' then assistant manager Jonatan Johansson became aware of the Colombian, and moves were made to bring him to Glasgow under then manager Pedro Caixinha.

The Morelos who arrived at Rangers in June 2017 is a much different player to the one whose last goal of the championship-winning season – a powerhouse of a left-footed effort which nearly took the Ibrox net and goal frame with it – came in a thumping 4-1 win against Celtic in April 2021.

Throughout Gerrard's first three seasons, Morelos fought off several more experienced contenders for his place in the starting 11, an attitude which showcases the forward's fighting spirit and desire to succeed. It's this iron will that carried him from the small town of Cereté in northern Colombia to Ibrox and international recognition, and still in his mid-20s, shows no sign of letting up.

Morelos enjoyed an excellent start to his Ibrox career, despite Rangers' misfortunes on the pitch in 2017/18. He finished his debut season with a respectable 18 goals as the lone striker in a 4-3-2-1 formation that was built to counter-attack and take advantage of his physical ability in the final third. A fiery, aggressive character who could become quickly drawn into altercations or distractions on the pitch, he was quickly identified as the type who – along with James Tavernier and Ryan Jack – could go on to excel in the type of environment Steven Gerrard was working hard to cultivate.

Throughout Gerrard's first season, Rangers were heavily reliant on Morelos as their primary goalscorer and he reached the landmark milestone of 30 goals in a suspension-hit campaign. Despite the addition of Hearts striker Kyle Lafferty, rejoining Rangers after a six-year absence and young Nigerian forward Umar Sadiq arriving on loan from AS Roma to provide competition for the Colombian, for multiple reasons, neither player could dethrone Morelos. It was not really until January 2019 signing Jermain Defoe joined that a viable alternative presented itself.

As with the purchases in Gerrard's first season, Rangers again looked to provide support to Morelos and share that goalscoring burden in the summer of 2020 with the captures of Kemar Roofe and Swiss striker Cedric Itten. Indeed, it was felt that these players would in fact be replacements for Morelos given the constant speculation around his future almost from the moment he set foot in Glasgow.

This was not to be, and all three forwards remained at the club as the transfer window closed. Itten and Roofe are very different players, but neither would provide direct competition for Morelos as the focal point of the attack. Roofe is undoubtedly capable of offering a similar skillset in certain situations but is not a direct replacement, whereas Itten was purchased as a striker used to playing in a 4-4-2 formation in Switzerland with St Gallen having finished with 23 goals in 2019/20. The Swiss was clearly a player who knew where the goal was. Despite this goalscoring ability, Itten's work outside the box was also of value as he showed his ability to work the channels and provide support to his team-mates. Never a consistent first pick within the team, Itten never looked like he really suited the tactical style in this season, and was mostly used off the bench where he would pop up with a couple of crucial goals, mostly against Motherwell.

Roofe and Morelos played together in the traditional new year Old Firm derby against Celtic, where Rangers won 1-0 and, looking back, all but sealed the 55th title. Coming into this game, Roofe was on a hot streak, having scored eight goals in his last eight games. Unfortunately he would succumb to injury just before half-time, but undeterred, Morelos would take up the mantle and lead the team to all but clinch the title in early March against St Mirren at Ibrox. From that Celtic game until St Mirren, Morelos would score seven goals and make five assists in just nine appearances. Having two strikers available – if not always playing together – was yet another key strand to this title-winning story.

Despite the contributions of both Morelos and Roofe when they featured in 2020/21, for the most part, Gerrard elected to use one or the other in his starting line-up, but rarely both.

Indeed, they played just eight times together in the league campaign.

2018/19 – Power

In the beginning, Morelos's style was all about raw, explosive power. While not blessed with top-level pace, his aggressive, combative style in his debut campaign – not dissimilar to Luis Suárez – would give him an advantage over most defenders on the ground. Playing as the team's number nine, Morelos displayed all the key characteristics you would expect from a lone striker in this role. On many occasions, Morelos would completely dominate two centre-backs on his own, playing a crucial role in creating chances for himself and, more importantly, utilising his physicality and close control to bring others into play.

He thrived on creating and taking advantage of the chaos on the pitch – in both the right and wrong ways – such was the nature of his attacking play. He could even be compared to Suárez right down to the way he seemed to almost kick the ball deliberately off defender's shins and gamble on his superior reactions to gain an advantage while they were disorientated.

Morelos had a natural tendency to drift into the right half-space when the team was attacking. This was evident throughout that first season as he linked well with James Tavernier and close friend Daniel Candeias on that side, encouraging both players to advance into attacking areas and create overloads from the centre of the pitch. A significant number of his goals would come from through balls in this area, with Morelos usually preferring to shoot – with often mixed results – as he entered the box from a narrow angle on the right. This ability to float into dangerous areas of the pitch was utilised more significantly in the seasons to come as his all-round game would begin to evolve, but it was clear as this season progressed that Rangers had uncovered a striker of high potential quality.

2019/20 – Record Breaker

The Colombian looked to be on track to break all kinds of records as he scored an incredible 28 goals before Christmas in his third season at the club. However, as would often be the case, things changed at the turn of the year as in the 11 games prior to the COVID shutdown in 2020 he would only add one more goal as his form and discipline tailed off in those difficult early months of the year. Morelos and Defoe remained as the number nines within the squad, aided by the addition of Swiss striker Florian Kamberi on loan in January to provide short-term backup following a rumoured failed move for Burnley striker Matěj Vydra.

The 'twin tens' tactical switch introduced in the latter stages of that first Gerrard season brought a significant additional focus on the value of combinations and positional rotation for the front three, and with that began the evolutions to Morelos's style of play.

Morelos saved his best performances for the Europa League in 2019/20, scoring an incredible 13 goals in 15 appearances, breaking the record for most goals scored in a season in the competition. Indeed, Morelos would score in five of the six group stage games with some genuinely memorable strikes, including a headed double away to Feyenoord and home and away strikes against Porto, with the goal at Ibrox in particular one of the best goals of his Rangers career, as he accepted a pass from Ryan Jack and allowed the ball to roll across his body before finishing with aplomb on his left into the bottom corner. Despite such an impressive goal record, Morelos did not display the killer instinct tendencies of a natural finisher and was more liable to score the difficult chances in bigger games than he was when clean through on goal in a one-on-one situation when given time to think. He is not a particularly clean striker of the ball either, with a tendency to scuff chances into the ground or attempt to blast the ball at goal when finesse finishes may be a better option. Despite a perceived clumsy and erratic shooting style at times, he can score with both feet, with that goal against Porto at Ibrox sumptuously put away on his weaker side.

Such is his physical presence and threat that defenders will naturally gravitate to him even when he drops deeper in the pitch, thus helping to create gaps in a team's defensive structure. This had two benefits to Rangers' overall offensive approach. Firstly, defenders will be drawn to Morelos, who could utilise his body to position himself between man and ball to win free kicks in dangerous areas, a crucial tactic for Rangers, particularly in Europe. This was especially true when faced with over-zealous defenders who want to either rile Morelos or nick the ball before he has a chance to cause any danger. Regardless, the role he played in gaining set-piece advantages in these areas cannot be overstated.

Secondly, while Morelos was not blessed with a fantastic range of passing or vision, he could create opportunities for team-mates and bring them into the game using other means. The introduction of players such as Joe Aribo and Ianis Hagi into the attacking areas in Gerrard's second season would provide Morelos with that support from deep to allow him to become more mobile, safe in the knowledge that other players would be in a position to attack the box at various points in the game.

With that, the improvement in his all-round game became more noticeable.

Figure 51

As with the overall Rangers tactical approach, risk vs reward was prevalent in Morelos's centre-forward play. At times, his movement off the ball in the box can be exceptional, particularly his ability to ghost in at the back post to take advantage of crosses from either full-back in the wide areas. Given Rangers' primary natural attacking width came from the full-backs, having a player who, while not a true aerial threat, can finish with his head was extremely advantageous.

MORELOS — LINK PLAY
Feyenoord 2-2 Rangers Europa League 28.11.19

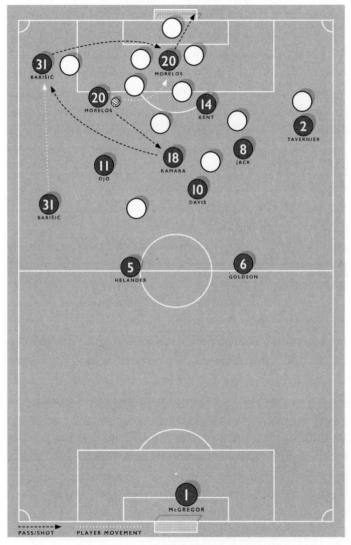

Morelos' movement off the ball and ability to find space at the back post provided Rangers with many avenues to attack.

FIGURE 51

In the Europa League group stage match away against Feyenoord in 2019, we saw a prime example of both his creation and finishing skills in one sweeping move. Morelos dropped deep in the left half-space to pick the ball up before sending the ball back to Glen Kamara in the middle of the Feyenoord half. Morelos signalled clearly for the ball to be returned to him, but instead Kamara elected to shift his weight and play a disguised pass to Borna Barišić, who had typically overloaded in space on the left-hand side. As soon as Kamara turned to make the pass, Morelos sprinted into the box in anticipation of the cross, positioning himself between both Feyenoord centre-backs. In typical Barišić style, the cross was pinpoint and delivered into the exact area Morelos had occupied. The Colombian executed a difficult looping header over the keeper and into the net to give Rangers a 2-1 lead on the night and put them in pole position to qualify from the group, something they would later go on to do.

2020 – False Nine

If Morelos could be compared to Luis Suárez in Gerrard's first season, his final evolution in the title-winning season would see his skillset being more closely aligned to that of another South American Liverpool forward, Brazil's Roberto Firmino. In a role widely acknowledged as being more of a 'false nine' than a traditional centre-forward, Morelos improved his ability in the build-up phase and was now much more capable as a creative player than the primary goalscorer of the first two seasons under Gerrard. In those campaigns, Morelos scored 59 goals in just 95 appearances. In 2020/21 Morelos made 44 appearances but scored just 17 goals, the lowest tally of his four years at the club. He had transformed into a false nine but still retained that ability to get into the box himself and score when the situation demanded it.

When asked about Morelos's role change from a traditional number nine to more of a playmaker, first-team coach Michael

Beale said on The Coaches' Voice, 'I think he's like a butterfly at times. When you play against a team that sit back on the edge of their box, he doesn't have the space that he had before to run down the sides. He does have it in Europe at times when teams face us more head on. It's the relationship between Alfredo and the other players [that has developed], if he comes short someone else goes long. We are allowing Alfredo to be the best version of himself. He's maturing, he's not a 21-year-old any more, he's a father and a little bit older now. My time in Brazil was fantastic for learning a little of the South American mentality and culture and that's helped me working with Alfredo.'

This role change was evident from the first game of the title-winning season, a 1-0 victory against Aberdeen at Pittodrie, with Morelos playing more noticeably as a withdrawn forward and combining effectively with Ryan Kent and Ianis Hagi in the attack. Indeed, Morelos would play a crucial role in the only goal, dropping deep into his half to collect a pass and slide the ball through the opposition defence for Kent to latch on to and score.

Another pertinent example of this would be the role of Morelos in a fairly routine victory against Ross County in early December 2020. The graphic illustrates the focus opposition defenders place on Alfredo and again nicely details how crucial third man runs are for Rangers to break teams down.

Figure 52 – Off-ball movement

This attack progressed all the way from Rangers' defensive third, through Calvin Bassey at left-back, and the ball found its way across to Ryan Kent, just inside the Rangers half. Kent drew pressure to himself before slipping the ball up to Morelos who had dropped off the front line into the right half-space, taking his marker with him. He faked playing a pass to the onrushing James Tavernier and instead funnelled the ball back to Steven Davis in central midfield. As he does so often, Davis played the perfect pass through the space Morelos had

MORELOS — OFF-BALL MOVEMENT
Ross County 0-4 Rangers SPFL 06.12.20

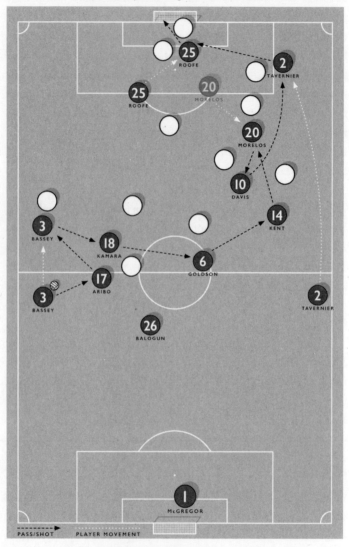

The evolution of Morelos could be summed up by his decisive contribution to this goal
as he dropped deep to create space for others to attack.

FIGURE 52

vacated to Tavernier, who had the room and time to slide a cross into the six-yard box, giving Kemar Roofe a relatively easy tap-in. To the naked eye, the praise would go to Davis's vision to make the pass or Tavernier's attacking ability to break through and find his man in the box, but Morelos made that goal possible with that movement to create the space for the pass. His ability on the ball in these situations is undervalued, too, particularly his ability to receive, control, and lay off short passes to team-mates.

It's a far cry from the physical domination of defenders in his first two years, but the team continued to benefit from his influence more often than not.

Morelos's well-documented disciplinary problems did also appear to be behind him as this season progressed. He was unavailable for 13 games in Gerrard's first two seasons due to red cards and accumulated suspension points, and in 2020/21 he missed just four games.

Pressing

With the final tactical evolution of the forward line seeing the continued utilisation of a much more fluid and dynamic combination of attackers, Morelos's role evolved further still. In specific scenarios during 2020/21, he would find himself on the left or right of the attack and would continue to play a significant role in the team's pressing strategy.

Figure 53 – Morelos initiating press

While more often acting as the team's focal point, Morelos was typically the first player to initiate the team's press when the opposition restart play. His role out of possession was heavily dependent on the level of opposition the team face. When Rangers were intent on winning the ball back in key areas, Morelos would advance on the centre-back in possession while positioning himself appropriately to take advantage of a pass into the other centre-back. He did this safe in the knowledge

MORELOS — INITIATING THE PRESS

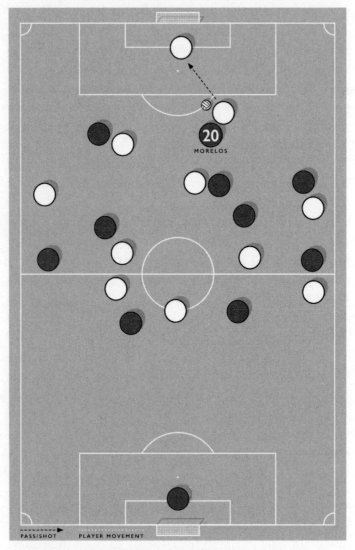

As the regular focal point of this Rangers team, Alfredo Morelos was often tasked with leading Rangers' pressing to restrict the opposition when building up from the back.

FIGURE 53

that the other two attackers will be well placed to capitalise on passes into the full-back areas.

If Rangers elected to stand off and revert into a mid-block, Morelos himself would do something similar and encourage the centre-back in possession to drive forward or attempt risky passes by positioning himself closer to the other centre-back and blocking the passing route.

As with the other attackers, Morelos's pressing ability became an attacking weapon when the opposition turn over possession as he was already in an advanced position and, given the nature of the player, was always likely to attempt a shot at goal if the opportunity presented itself.

There was a debate that becoming a more rounded footballer as Morelos undoubtedly did and tempering his natural aggressive streak on the pitch potentially stunted that edge to his game he became famous for, as he was no longer the Colombian whirlwind who seemed to take on entire defences at will during his first two years at the club. He is now more mature as a man and a footballer. Like Suárez, he seems to thrive on playing on the line – and sometimes stepping over it – but when you take that away, they can perhaps lose a little of what made them such a key player.

Looking at it from another angle, Rangers evolved to a point where they were now no longer as heavily reliant on Morelos to be that player. Several members of the squad could share the goalscoring burden, which may have played a part in his desire to improve his all-round game. Regardless, his new-found maturity on the field also coincided with his change in tactical role, but the fact undoubtedly remains that the evolution of Morelos was yet another key in Rangers' team during the title-winning season.

Signature Goals

It's often said that certain teams score goals that sum up their playing philosophy so perfectly that they could be classed as their 'signature goals'. In my head, this usually takes me back to Barcelona under Pep Guardiola and the way Xavi and Iniesta would combine almost telepathically, searching for the split-second weakness in a team's defensive structure that would allow them to slip a perfectly weighted pass through to Messi to invariably score and invariably on his left foot.

Or maybe, to use a more recent example of a Guardiola team, Manchester City. How many times did we see City open teams up using combinations on the right wing which resulted in a low cross flashed across goal for Raheem Sterling to slide the ball into an empty net? Or the full-back to full-back combinations at Liverpool between Andy Robertson and Trent-Alexander Arnold?

Throughout this book I have attempted to illustrate what I feel are the important tactical and philosophical details that produced Rangers' success during Gerrard's three full seasons in charge. It will come as no surprise to anyone that when a coaching staff look to implement such a highly structured, well-coached tactical set-up there is a huge amount of work done on the training pitch working on every forensic detail. These goals are borne from constant repetition of patterns of play to achieve as close to perfection on the football pitch as is humanly possible.

With that in mind, it's only natural that a Rangers team that could be so well identified by its 4-3-2-1 formation on the pitch would look to repeat these patterns during games, and do so with great success. In this section, I have picked out what I consider to be five 'signature goals' that sum up Rangers' tactical philosophy and highlight just how important each single action by each player can be and when they dovetail together as intended, can create some fantastic goals that will long be etched in the memory of every Rangers fan.

Figure 54

As outlined in earlier chapters, a key aim of Rangers' attacking play was focused on building up attacks through the right-hand side of the pitch before switching play quickly to Borna Barišić to allow him to deliver into the box. This goal is one of the best examples of this and not only did it come in one of the biggest domestic games of the 2019/20 season, it helped to deliver Rangers' first victory at Parkhead in ten years, another key step in the journey back to the top of Scottish football.

In the 36th minute of the first half and with the score at 0-0, Rangers won the ball back deep in their own right-back area of the pitch through a combination of Ryan Jack and Steven Davis. The latter showcased all of his skills in possession to initiate a series of quick passes between himself, Joe Aribo and Glen Kamara which not only saw Rangers break through Celtic's line of counter-pressure, but enabled Aribo to find Alfredo Morelos on the right side of the attack. The Colombian had successfully managed to isolate Celtic centre-back Christopher Jullien and – with the aid of a deflection – was able to find Kamara in a central position. Kamara did what he does best and moved the ball quickly and efficiently across pitch while dragging Celtic players out of their defensive line as the overload began to take shape. Jack received the pass and played a quick one touch pass to Barišić who had been left in ten yards of space due to Celtic's defence being pulled to the opposite side of the park.

Barišić's improved cross variation is again evident here as the expectation is that he would attempt to hit the byline and

SIGNATURE GOAL — THE OVERLOAD
Celtic 1-2 Rangers SPFL 29.12.19

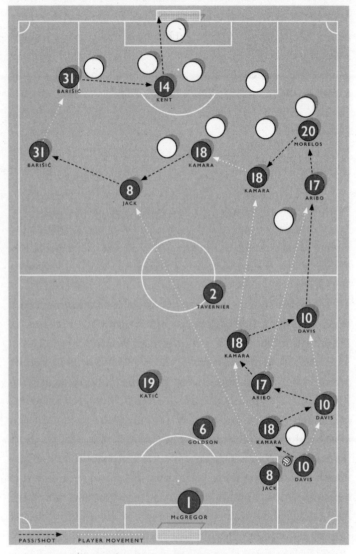

Rangers would regularly build attacks down their right-hand side before switching quickly to the opposite flank to make use of Borna Barisic's crossing ability.

FIGURE 54

cross into the box. With the aid of a stepover, he was able to disguise a pull-back to the centre of the box and an unmarked Kent who delivered an outstanding one-touch left-footed finish to give Rangers a 1-0 lead. Rangers' ability to move the ball at speed was a key factor in this goal, but the movement of players such as Aribo and Kamara to drag opposition defenders into non-threatening areas was just as vital as this created the opportunity to overload and gave Kent the freedom required to score.

Figure 55

There were some incredibly crucial European goals throughout Steven Gerrard's management, but none more so than the goals that delivered Rangers' safe passage into the group stage of the Europa League thus giving the club the financial platform to recruit players of significant quality to move on to the next level. First, there was Ovie Ejaria's lovely finish in Russia against FC Ufa in August 2018. In 2019, a stunning injury-time header from Alfredo Morelos was enough to progress past Legia Warsaw at Ibrox.

The most impressive victory in qualifying, however, was saved for the title-winning season with Rangers defeating Turkish giants Galatasaray 2-1 in a one-legged qualifying round. Given the magnitude of the game, you would struggle to find two more aesthetically pleasing goals with the first scored by Scott Arfield and the second by James Tavernier. Tavernier's goal is another example of Rangers' overload on the left and has been covered in great detail earlier in this book. Arfield's showcased how Rangers again utilised the 'third man run' tactical concept to great effect.

Tavernier picked the ball up in the right half-space and played a quick entry pass into the feet of Morelos, who had dropped into space. By doing so, Morelos was looking to receive the pass, but he also dragged Galatasaray's Brazilian centre-back Marcão out of the defensive line. Morelos dummied this

SIGNATURE GOAL – THE THIRD MAN RUN

Rangers 2-1 Galatasaray Europa League 01.10.20

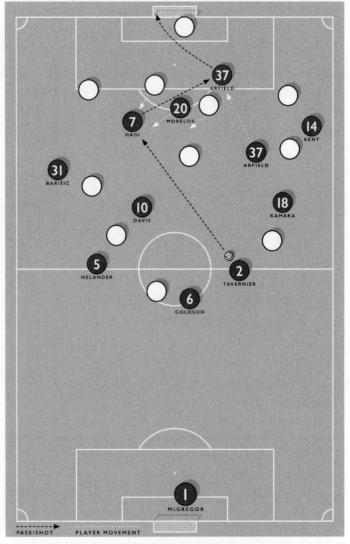

PASS/SHOT   PLAYER MOVEMENT

Scott Arfield and Ianis Hagi would combine several times in the early months of season 2020/21 using the third man run concept, including this opening goal against Galatasaray at Ibrox.

FIGURE 55

pass, allowing it to run through to Ianis Hagi, who displayed his excellent vision and passing by taking one touch, then threading a pass into the space left by Marcão into which Arfield had run. As the move happened so quickly, the Galatasaray left-back Martin Linnes was unable to tuck in to cover this run and Arfield was able to break into the box and score with the outside of his right foot.

Just five touches between three players and Rangers had sliced Galatasaray open with a wonderful goal that sent them on their way to a crucial victory and the Europa League group stages for the third year running.

Figure 56

As part of the meticulous approach by the management team, no marginal gain was left uncovered and none more so than set pieces. In 2020/21 Rangers would score from no fewer than nine corners, which was one fewer than the ten scored in 2019/20 but a significant increase on the five in 2018/19. Ask any Rangers fan, and the team's ability from set pieces had long been much maligned, so the work done by defensive coach Tom Culshaw allowed the team to reap significant rewards in this area.

Speaking in October 2019, Gerrard told *The Scotsman* of Culshaw's influence on Rangers' set-piece routines, 'I have to give a lot of credit to Tom Culshaw. He works so hard and puts a lot of effort into small details to make sure from an attacking point of view the delivery is right. He deserves a lot of credit for the goals we scored.'

The outswinging cross was usually favoured by both left- and right-sided corner takers due to the disadvantage this puts the goalkeeper at, as he would not want to overcommit and come for a cross he may not be able to collect, thus leaving the attack with an open goal. An outswinger of this nature also allows the attacking players to run on to the ball and generate maximum power to direct the header goalwards. An example of this could be seen in the 2-1 victory at Parkhead

SIGNATURE GOAL - THE SET PIECE
Celtic 1-1 Rangers SPFL 21.03.21

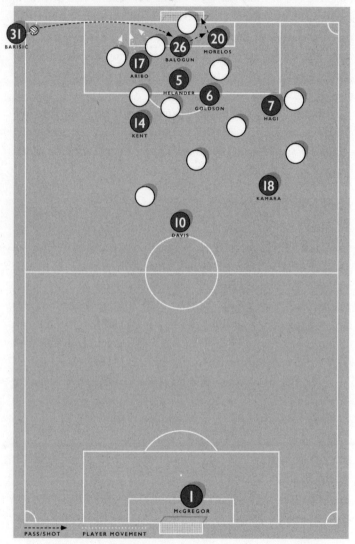

This set piece routine was one of Rangers most successful under Gerrard. Joe Aribo's near post run and flick on was key to stretching the defence thus creating space at the back post for Morelos to score.

FIGURE 56

258

in December 2019, with Niko Katić's bullet header clinching victory for Rangers.

The routine depicted here is the most easily recognisable, given it yielded no fewer than three goals in Old Firm games during Gerrard's tenure, including the one just mentioned. In this example, Borna Barišić is tasked with delivering an outswinging ball into the box.

The cross variation used is an important factor also as opposition defences still expect the ball to be thrown into the six-yard box for centre-backs to try and connect with. On this occasion and several others, the near-post run of Aribo is crucial as not only does this drag the defending team out of position, Aribo's height ensures he dominates regularly at the near post, thus getting first connection on the ball and sending it into the danger area. In this example, Aribo made that run to create space but it was Leon Balogun who connected with the ball. The role of Morelos in corner routines was also crucial, with the Colombian usually starting in the centre of the goal but immediately peeling to the back post to anticipate the flick-on across goal. In this example, that flick came and Morelos was able to convert into an empty net for his first goal in an Old Firm derby.

Figure 57

An interesting comment levied at Rangers throughout this period was their ability to consistently achieve results against teams in Europe, while seeming to struggle more in domestic games they should be expected to win quite comfortably. It was a complete contrast to watching Rangers in the 1990s when I was growing up as this was a glorious domestic era where they famously won nine titles in a row yet would regularly exit European competition to teams such as Levski Sofia, AEK Athens and RC Strasbourg before the clocks went back. It was felt then that despite Rangers' domestic dominance, they simply could not match up to most European teams tactically, due to

SIGNATURE GOAL – THE COUNTER ATTACK
Rangers 5-2 Antwerp Europa League 25.02.21

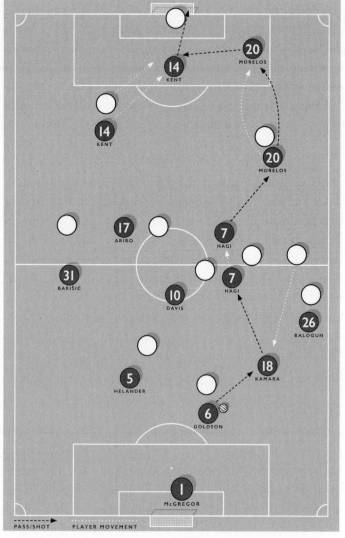

Rangers' devastating ability to counter-attack was particularly crucial during their Europa League campaigns.

FIGURE 57

the ever-increasing chasm in finances and the perceived total change in style required to play at that level.

A similar task faced Steven Gerrard but straight from the off, Rangers were able to adapt to the European stage with ease and indeed seemed to revel in the tactical battles that ensued. Having less of the ball in Europe than Rangers do in Scotland is always more likely to happen given the calibre of teams that visited Ibrox in this period, but Rangers used this to their advantage several times with the execution of some truly stunning counter-attacking goals.

In an incredible end-to-end last-32 tie in the 2020/21 Europa League, Rangers beat Royal Antwerp 4-3 in the first leg in Belgium before a 5-2 victory at Ibrox that saw the team advance in emphatic style. Rangers' third goal on the night, scored by Ryan Kent, showcased exactly how the teams' counter-attacks had evolved and developed into a devastating weapon.

With the score at 2-1, Glen Kamara dropped into the right-back position to pick the ball up from Connor Goldson and looked to build an attack. He played what should have been a relatively safe pass into the feet of Ianis Hagi but the Romanian's quick thinking and excellent movement turned this from seemingly sterile possession into something much more dangerous. Hagi could never be described as quick across the grass, but he more than made up for that with speed of thought and an excellent first touch. Both of these things combined beautifully as he span away from two Antwerp players with his first touch and released a pass to Morelos with his second.

Given the score and Antwerp's need to attack, this movement left Morelos and Kent man for man with two Antwerp defenders. Morelos – always so dangerous in that right half-space when facing up a defender – produced another moment of magic as he drew the defender in then passed the ball past him while running around the other side to retrieve the ball and advance into the box. From there he was able to flash a first-time ball across goal which found Ryan Kent, who made a fantastic run on the blind side of the defender to smash the ball home via the goalkeeper's outstretched hand. With just three passes Rangers had taken the ball from their own defence to the back of the Antwerp net in just nine seconds to seal the victory and their place in the last 16.

Figure 58

The final signature goal fittingly comes from the final game of Rangers' title-winning season. In this example, Rangers used the counter-pressing approach that was honed on the training pitch to significant effect against Aberdeen at Ibrox. Despite this being the final game of the season and all eyes on the imminent receipt of the championship trophy, Rangers' relentless thirst for goals was clear for all to see. Immediately following an Aberdeen attack, Rangers attempted to hit quickly on the counter-attack through James Tavernier, who played a ball into the right-hand channel. Aberdeen were able to recover possession once more but as mentioned in the 'Own the Ball' section earlier in this book, Rangers' continued use of counter-pressing came to the fore here as they again tried to recover the loose ball and create a dangerous attack. In this instance, Aberdeen were able to retain possession, but you can see how narrow and compact the three Rangers attackers were despite the fraught nature of play at this stage of the game. Morelos as the lone striker and the focal point of the attack was then able to re-apply pressure on the Aberdeen defender, causing him to play a risky pass into a dangerous area of the pitch.

This was intercepted well by Hagi, who had remained close to Morelos but narrow on the pitch with the aim of pressing should the situation require it. Hagi gained possession of the ball and quickly distributed it to Kemar Roofe in what Michael Beale refers to as the 'defensive red zone' due to the likelihood that the opposition will be able to create a high-quality chance

SIGNATURE GOAL – THE COUNTER PRESS
Rangers 4-0 Aberdeen SPFL 15.05.21

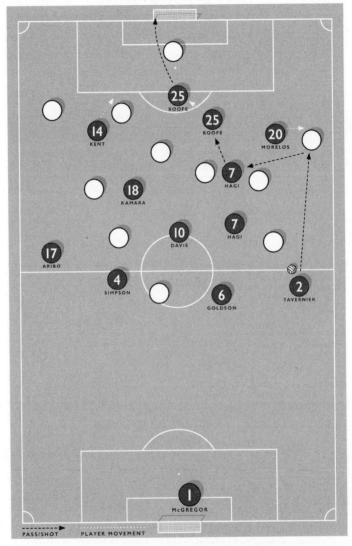

The front three's ability to work as a team to counter-press the opposition and force mistakes in their defensive line was apparent throughout the whole season, including the final-day victory against Aberdeen.

FIGURE 58

so close to the goal. The counter-press had caught Aberdeen unaware and their defensive structure had been completely torn apart, leaving Roofe to score Rangers' penultimate league goal of the campaign with relative ease.

2021/22

Throughout summer 2021, the incredible high experienced by all of a Rangers persuasion seemed as if it would carry on forever. The pressure of winning the title had finally lifted, but did the hunger and appetite to come back for more go with it? This was a squad who had been together for two or three years at this point and together with the management team had achieved their stated aim when they were appointed to the club. In modern football, not many teams stay together for much longer than a four- or five-year period whether that it due to poor performance resulting in managerial sackings, players being sold or quite the opposite. Sometimes, unprecedented success brings offers way beyond your wildest dreams, and players will naturally move on. You only have to look at the Ajax team who made it all the way to the Champions League semi-final in 2019 as an example of how clubs from outside the top five leagues can be picked apart by those with greater financial resources.

As it was, Rangers retained all of their key players and the general consensus was that the squad was more than strong enough to embark on another successful season.

A stop-start pre-season with several injuries and suspensions couldn't have been further from the seamless start to the season prior but the club closed off their preparations with a fantastic day at Ibrox as Rangers beat Real Madrid 2-1 in a glamour friendly in late July, with new Zambian international striker Fashion Sakala bagging the opener. There were some major early season disappointments as Rangers exited the Champions League qualifiers by way of losing to Swedish champions Malmö 4-2 on aggregate and being beaten 1-0 by Dundee United in just their second league game of the season. The club qualified for the Europa League group stages for the fourth season running – a successful achievement in its own right given how crucial European funds had been to Rangers' rebuild – courtesy of a nervy 1-0 aggregate victory over Armenian champions Alashkert.

Following a 4-2 win against Ross County on 7 November 2021, Rangers were four points ahead of Celtic in the league as autumn started to move into winter and the league campaign closed down for the final international break of the year. The team had not reached the heights of the previous season, conceding 13 goals in their first 13 games, a huge difference from the season previous when just 13 were conceded in the entire campaign. Despite this, the news emanating from Ibrox in the next few days would come as a huge shock to everyone associated with the club as it was announced just four days later that Steven Gerrard and the majority of his backroom staff had accepted an offer to take over the management of Aston Villa following the departure of Dean Smith.

And there ended Steven Gerrard's story as Rangers manager. He delivered the title he promised he would deliver and brought Rangers back to the summit of Scottish football, something which deserved huge celebration, particularly when you consider the rebuilding job undertaken in summer 2018.

Epilogue

I HOPE you enjoyed reading this book as much as I have enjoyed writing it. Rangers' 55th title was the culmination of three years of incremental improvements to the playing squad, an unfailing belief in a tactical philosophy and a trust in key players to deliver when needed. It may have been a three-year project, but that one day in March 2021 when Rangers were crowned champions in record-breaking time helped to banish ten years of hurt firmly to the history books.

The entire team and coaching staff who delivered 55 will be forever etched in the history of the club, and rightly so. What they achieved over the course of the three years was exceptional, with the league championship trophy coming back to Ibrox being the pinnacle of this. Regardless of what they go on to do in football, this was a special team who found themselves in a special moment, something that football fans and fans of the sport, in general, should always celebrate.

55 Times the Kings of Scotland

Bibliography

Reference

https://www.heraldscotland.com/news/16206751.dave-king-
    rights-issue-isnt-critical-rangers---funding-will-made-
    available-steven-gerrard/

https://www.rangers.co.uk/article/rangers-coaches-
    convention-announced/29g4YRN3b0icx9nrFEANrO

https://www.rangers.co.uk/article/rangers-coaches-
    convention-announced/29g4YRN3b0icx9nrFEANrO

https://www.rangers.co.uk/article/rangers-coaches-
    convention-announced/29g4YRN3b0icx9nrFEANrO

https://www.liverpoolecho.co.uk/sport/football/football-
    news/steven-gerrard-rodgers-benitez-klopp-19661361

Jamie Carragher's The Greatest Game podcast: https://
    podcasts.apple.com/gb/podcast/10-steven-gerrard/
    id1483757361?i=1000461975039

https://www.scotsman.com/sport/football/rangers/steven-
    gerrard-reveals-rangers-and-liverpool-similarities-and-
    why-ibrox-side-can-go-toe-toe-any-club-britain-3135482

https://www.mirror.co.uk/sport/football/news/gerrard-
    rangers-klopp-liverpool-lfc-23763855

https://michaelbealecoaching.com/2020/03/24/the-coaches-
    that-inspire-me/

Robbie Fowler Podcast: https://podcasts.apple.com/gb/
podcast/steven-gerrard/id1547826633?i=1000509083904

https://www.90min.com/posts/ross-wilson-rangers-
interview-sporting-director-steven-gerrard

https://www.90min.com/posts/ross-wilson-rangers-
interview-sporting-director-steven-gerrard

https://www.rangers.co.uk/article/rangers-coaches-
convention-announced/29g4YRN3b0icx9nrFEANrO

https://www.liverpoolfc.com/news/behind-the-
badge/289911-tom-culshaw-steven-gerrard-
liverpool-u18s

https://trainingground.guru/staff-profiles/aston-villa-
staff-profiles

https://www.pressreader.com/uk/the-sunday-post-newcast
le/20210207/283068417002334

Robbie Fowler Podcast: https://podcasts.apple.com/gb/
podcast/steven-gerrard/id1547826633?i=1000509083904

https://www.coachesvoice.com/rangers-coach-michael-
beale-steven-gerrard-liverpool-chelsea/

https://www.coachesvoice.com/rangers-coach-michael-
beale-steven-gerrard-liverpool-chelsea/

https://www.coachesvoice.com/rangers-coach-michael-
beale-steven-gerrard-liverpool-chelsea/

https://www.rangers.co.uk/article/relentle55-the-movie-
launches-today/5rAlO1lqAFPsDkhPX8BMuq

https://www.rangers.co.uk/article/exclusive-scott-mason-
interview/5XrL1uaOOhuIJLQsdzbvVQ

https://www.rangers.co.uk/article/exclusive-scott-mason-
interview/5XrL1uaOOhuIJLQsdzbvVQ

https://academy.coachesvoice.com/programs/cv-live-
michael-beale-on-demand

https://academy.coachesvoice.com/programs/cv-live-michael-beale-on-demand

https://academy.coachesvoice.com/programs/cv-live-michael-beale-on-demand

https://www.thisisanfield.com/2017/04/obsessed-steven-gerrard-become-great-player/

https://academy.coachesvoice.com/programs/cv-live-michael-beale-on-demand

https://academy.coachesvoice.com/programs/cv-live-michael-beale-on-demand

https://academy.coachesvoice.com/programs/cv-live-michael-beale-on-demand

https://michaelbealecoaching.com/2019/03/22/outplay-your-direct-opponent/

https://academy.coachesvoice.com/programs/cv-live-michael-beale-on-demand

https://traininggroundguru.podbean.com/e/26-michael-beale-rangers-renaissance/

https://podcasts.apple.com/gb/podcast/steven-gerrard-how-to-make-high-expectations-a-reality/id1500444735?i=1000496057471

https://www.pressreader.com/uk/scottish-daily-mail/20200302/283446373479549

https://www.bbc.co.uk/sport/football/44795834

https://www.worldsoccer.com/best-of-ws/player-biography-blaise-matuidi-410652

https://www.youtube.com/watch?v=6umo--lyYxI
Rangers Relentless Video

https://www.forbes.com/sites/zakgarnerpurkis/2021/01/29/the-secret-injury-advantage-behind-rangers-23-point-scottish-premier-league-lead/

Rangers Relentless Video

https://www.glasgowtimes.co.uk/sport/19154749.happy-days-allan-mcgregor-describes-last-gasp-wonder-save-earned-rangers-draw-slavia-prague/

https://www.thescottishsun.co.uk/sport/football/2921938/rangers-steven-gerrard-careless-ross-mccrorie/

https://www.scotsman.com/sport/football/rangers/latest-rangers-news/rangers-coach-pinpoints-player-who-has-made-difference-team-1418706

https://www.scotsman.com/sport/football/steven-gerrard-i-was-jealous-ryan-jacks-performance-269406

https://theathletic.com/1992720/2020/08/13/jackamara-celticish-rangers-kamara-jack/

https://www.thescottishsun.co.uk/sport/football/4484559/rangers-filip-helander-steven-gerrard/

https://www.rangers.co.uk/article/gerrard-praises-jermain-defoe-and-cedric-itten/2HrpnUTobD3m7uKHvNTw4f

https://theathletic.com/1916695/2020/07/16/rangers-midfield-gerrard-aribo-davis-beale-kamara-jack/

https://www.theguardian.com/football/blog/2016/aug/18/the-question-kevin-de-bruyne-silva-free-roles

https://www.scotsman.com/sport/football/rangers/latest-rangers-news/rangers-coach-pinpoints-player-who-has-made-difference-team-1418706

https://www.heraldscotland.com/sport/19521546.rangers-close-midfield-addition-steven-gerrard-addresses-ibrox-transfer-business/

RangersTV

https://academy.coachesvoice.com/programs/cv-live-michael-beale-on-demand

https://www.scotsman.com/sport/football/rangers/latest-
rangers-news/could-rangers-set-piece-puppet-master-be-
difference-scottish-premiership-title-race-celtic-1403884